A Believer's Guide to

THE LAW OF ATTRACTION:

A Scriptural Map for Transformation

and Manifesting God's Destiny in Your Life

Robin Perry Braun, M.Psy.

TABLE OF CONTENTS

Chapter

ACKNOWLEDGMENTS

It becomes difficult to name people who have impacted you over the course of twenty years, there are too many to name. The fire for my passion about the content of this book was ignited first by the lifetime work of John and Paula Sandford, perhaps two of the boldest pioneers in inner healing ever. More contemporarily my deepest gratitude goes to Dr. George Burriss, II Ph.D. His passion to ground The Law of Attraction in scripture fueled me to find more answers in my quest. He is one of the most gifted teachers I have had the pleasure to sit under.

Thanks to Mark Braun for the editing and needed encouragement and all my friends who were brave enough to read my work in progress and comment. Thanks to Deborah Fisher for the amazing cover design and typesetting. Thanks to Ken and Tonia for giving me a space in this season to complete this work.

INTRODUCTION

In the past couple of years, I have been hearing more and more people talk about "Quantum Physics" and the "Law of Attraction" as they apply to everyday life. God had already been leading me on a journey to learn more about this principle. He was clearly guiding my steps from every direction and there has been a sense of destiny for me to pursue a deeper understanding of the principles of Quantum Physics as they apply to living a life as a believer in Christ. I was searching for missing puzzle pieces. I have been involved in inner healing and ministry for more than 20 years but saw something missing in people finding lasting freedom and transformation. They would receive some healing or transformation after a session or workshop but days, weeks, months later, they had the same issues once again. I was one of those people. With all my education, knowledge and healing experiences both personal and professional, why was I still struggling in certain areas? As I read literature, researched online, etc., I realized I had been using most of these principles in ministry for years but they were only taught to me in a scriptural/spiritual context. They were the same truths, but using different lingo, I began to learn a new context in which to apply them and some deeper applications which I felt provided pieces to this healing puzzle.

Often when I broach the topic with other Christians, they either have no idea what I am saying they remark, "Quantum Physics? Law of Attraction? Isn't that New Age? That's not in the Bible." In those situations, I'm comforted by remembering the process which all significant truths undergo, known as the Universal Three Stages of Truth as described by the German Philosopher Arthur Schopenhauer (1788-1860)[i]

1. It is mocked and ridiculed.
2. It is violently opposed.
3. It is accepted as self-evident.

The Christian Church historically throws out anything that other streams of spirituality have embraced. I believe this is because of a fear of being deceived. Yet Truth ultimately comes from God and may be expressed through channels unfamiliar to us and our worldview or particular denominational vantage point. If only the Church had the security in their walk with God and intimacy with the Holy Spirit to mine Truth from all sources, validate it with scripture and understand its application in our lives. God wants us to heal and mature and He releases revelation in the season it is needed, but He often confounds the boxes and formulas we create, He may choose to use "the foolish to confound the wise." (1 Corinthians 1:27). We can become very religious if we think God only speaks through and gives understanding to born-again believers. If that's the case, we need to throw out much of the minute-by-minute science and technology we apply every day.

I would like to share a little bit about my journey. In high school, I struggled with my self-image and became obsessed with my body image which led to a long battle with anorexia/bulimia and thus to seek out personal healing and transformation. After a few years of tenaciously pursuing it, I was completely healed and set free from this obsession (which is very rare statistically speaking). In 1986, I accepted Christ as my savior in a church service in Atlanta. I have been a student of inner healing and Christian counseling for the past 20+ years. I hold a Bachelor's in Psychology and Biblical Studies and a Masters degree in Clinical Psychology. I am certified in Elijah House, Restoring the Foundations, Vision Life Ministries, and Exchanged Life Christian Counseling. I am in the process of having both a Licensed Chemical Dependency Counselor's and a Licensed Professional Counselor's licensures. I have volunteered and worked in a variety of Christian modalities and settings, including Addiction Ministries, a Christian In-patient Adolescent Christian Treatment Center, and a variety of Churches. I have a growing private practice and teach an integrated Holistic approach to healing (and I am seeing tremendous results) to anyone who will listen. I believe God designed our incredible bodies to stay healthy and heal themselves, if we can identify the source of stress that is causing sickness and remove it. He does indeed heal miraculously but the disease/illness may return if we don't find the root cause.

It has been my life's pursuit to find the best modalities of healing for the wounds in Christians. While I have seen many instant healings of physical issues, I have witnessed few truly instantaneous healings of wounded hearts and these seem to occur little by little in relational settings. Since, the wounding occurred in relationships; God tends to bring healing in relational ways.

In my own journey and from observing that of many others, I have discovered missing pieces in many of the modalities I have seen and experienced. I believe that the truths behind The Law of Attraction, which I will correlate to Biblical principles, provide some very significant missing pieces to the healing of the whole person --body, soul and spirit. I hope to shed some light on these principles. Ultimately my goal is not just to educate you of the Biblical validity of Quantum Physics principles but also to show how useful The Law of Attraction truly can be in application to the wounds of our souls and hearts,

In preparation for writing this book, I bought *Quantum Physics for Dummies*. What an oxymoron! I expected a book using layman's terms of the principles about Quantum Physics that I had learned from other avenues. What I discovered was a book that required an IQ of at least 190 to even decipher the formulas and code on most of the pages. I suppose in the field of Quantum Physics, the term "dummy" is very relative. My copy of this book is now for resale on Amazon.com.

Quantum Physics is one of the most researched topics currently on search engines. Consequently, this is a "now" book and one of the top search engine phrases. I believe you will find answers to both an understanding of the Law of Attraction but, more specifically, a Biblical basis for its veracity AND a "how to apply" to your own life for transformation.

It saddens me how the metaphysical Church recognizes the power in all truth and applies it to their lives, yet are rejected by mainstream Christianity because they may be too broad and inclusive for our comfort level and theology. Scripture is our plumb line even if we don't all agree about various Biblical doctrines. The Holy Spirit reveals truth to our innermost parts if we will spend our life seeking to know Him at this deep level of intimacy. I believe the Church's core issue is not primarily a problem of doctrines but an intimacy disorder (at least in my American Church experience).

As believers in the Lord Jesus Christ, filled with the Holy Spirit, we have access to the clearest or most direct pathway to truth and the power of God. Consequently we should all be experiencing wellness-- physically, emotionally and spiritually. We should be walking in peace and joy. Proverbs 4:18 *"But the path of the righteous is like the light of dawn, which shines brighter and brighter until full day."* Yet in my experience, Christians seem to have as many or more problems than the rest of the world. Currently, we are not very salty and our light is not as bright as evidenced by such a quick declining church base and a lack of the fruit of the spirit in the lives of the general population of believers. It has been my life's pursuit to know why and be an instrument of healing.

CHAPTER 1

BASICS OF QUANTUM PHYSICS AND
THE LAW OF ATTRACTION

Quantum Physics cannot be easily taught or explained in purely scientific terms. I am certain that a minimum IQ of genius is required to understand the math. You can find short videos on *YouTube* that do the best job at keeping it understandable. Grasping these basic paradigmatic principles will alter the way you view

the world, thought, speech, time and life. Everything shared is easily verified online, so you can research in depth if you desire. The topic is quite fascinating.

The definition of *Quantum Physics*, a.k.a. *Quantum Mechanics* is the study of the smallest particles of physical phenomena. Specifically, it looks at atomic and subatomic particles and waves from all sources of matter. Research in this field has been a main focus of grant money over the past couple of decades and even more recently, as technology has produced methods for accurately measuring movement of small particles. For our purposes, I will detail three basic truths that have now been proven scientifically.

Truth #1

The first truth is that everything is made up of atoms and particles, which are energy. We already knew this to be true because we have been studying atoms for decades. But there wasn't much talk about the conclusions. If everything is comprised of atoms, then all humans are made up of energy and only a small part of us is actually solid matter. We know that the majority of an atom is simply empty space in motion. In fact, did you realize over 99.99% of an atom is space? The illusion of having more matter is only because it is in motion. For example, if you move a flashing light between two points quickly, it gives the illusion of a line, but in reality, it is a series of dots.

So this: |-- -|
When it is in motion, looks like this:

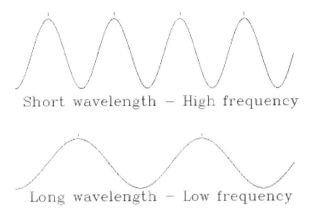

Short wavelength — High frequency

Long wavelength — Low frequency

This means that you and I are essentially a hologram. Years ago, when I saw the movie *The Matrix* for the first time, something shifted deep inside me that I could not articulate. Somehow I knew, maybe for the first time, that the world I saw was an illusion and the real world was the spirit realm. It shifted my faith and I often meditate on this concept when I am "stuck in the trees and can't see the forest." Do you ever find yourself in this same place? Those great heroes of faith whom I admire seem to live this idea and are not moved by circumstances or what they see. Remember **Hebrews 11:1**, *"Now **faith** is the substance **of things** hoped for, **the evidence of things not seen**.* Imagine if we could truly think, on a regular basis, that everything around us is a hologram and the only true reality is spiritual and our consciousness of what we see. (The way we see the hologram because the hologram is not real.) I imagine we would live life very differently.

Historically, Hollywood seems to have a pulse on what God is doing in the universe and they often (albeit unknowingly) prophesy about it. If we look at many of the movies in the past years, we find the topics of time travel, dream states, other realities and more. There is a principle of Quantum Physics related to this concept of consciousness, but is not the topic of this book. Wrapping our brains around the idea that we are more than 99.99% empty space is not just material for blonde jokes. Given the current development or movement towards energy medicine and healing, it simply makes good scientific sense to learn more about this idea that we are made up of energy. Learning a new paradigm about vibration and energy is exciting but challenging because it seems to violate most of our past paradigms. I encourage you to brave this journey as you see how Quantum Physics is grounded in the Word of God. I am confident God will bring revelation to you along the way. I still don't have my finite brain wrapped around most of the Quantum Physics discoveries, yet like eating an elephant, I just take one bite at a time. To repeat, **Truth #1 says we are all made up of atoms and thus made up of energy.**

Truth #2

The second truth is that *all energy vibrates and gives off a frequency that is measured at a certain wavelength.* Different energies create different wavelengths or frequencies. High frequency means that the peaks of the wavelengths are close together and occur more often. Low frequency means that the peaks of the wavelengths are farther apart and occur less often.

Wavelength is usually measured not in meters (m) but in smaller parts of a meter (smaller than a millimeter or the width of a dime) Frequency is *the number of cycles of a wave to pass some point in a second.* The units of frequency are thus cycles per second, or Hertz (Hz). Radio stations have frequencies. They are usually equal to the station number times 1,000,000 Hz. For instance, if a radio station has the FM band of 94.9 then it is 94.9 million Hz. Did you know that electromagnetic waves can not only be described by their wavelength, but also by their energy and frequency? All three of these things are **related to each other mathematically.**

There has been understanding about sound wavelengths for many decades. When you turn on your radio and go to 94.9 – that is a frequency that your radio is finding. That radio station is sending its signal out on that frequency. When you tune into the same frequency, you pick up the signal. The frequency can only travel so many miles depending on the strength of the projector/tower that is sending the signal. The same principle applies with television, cell phone and all the technology that we ignorantly take for granted every day. But it also works in and thru us! We only know it works to send sound and pictures across a certain span. Satellites in space can cover greater territory than towers on the earth.

We all know that dogs hear a greater range of frequency than the human ear does. That is why a dog whistle agitates a dog yet we hear nothing. Our eardrum does not pick up the frequency of the whistle so it does not vibrate when the whistle is blown. How amazing is our human body that our ear works like a receiver that sends signals to the brain to turn wavelengths into words, harmonies, etc.? God created us as a walking satellite, sending and receiving signals or frequencies. Did you know that Einstein knew this at the turn of the century? He theorized that the human brain operated as a two way satellite, sending and receiving signals.

Our eyes see because of frequencies also. Colors have different wavelengths as well. A rainbow is light that is separated into its different frequencies. Our finely tuned eye can distinguish hundreds even thousands of nuances in color along with shape, size etc. Both of these organs function as receptors of frequency.

Did you know that smells all have distinct frequencies also? Our nose picks up the frequency and transmits it to the brain. Did you know that in the field of aromatherapy that different essential oils (oils made from the essence of a plant/flower etc.) directly affect the brain by the frequency they transmit? Our brain reacts to these frequencies by sending different signals to the body. The scientific developments in this field are other amazing facts to research. This is another example of areas that the more metaphysical and New Age arenas have embraced for years and the mainstream population is only now accepting because it can be proven scientifically. **So truth #2 is that all energy vibrates and gives off a frequency.**

Truth #3

The third truth is that *wavelengths or frequencies attract similar or like wavelengths or frequencies.* The waves are biogmagnetic in nature so they attract like frequencies as would a magnet. So, high frequency Hz attracts like Hz and low frequency Hz attracts low frequency Hz as well. **The challenge to explain these principles scientifically is very complex.** In reality, magnets attract opposite charges. Positive attracts negative electromagnetic waves. This book is focused on the practical application of the Law of Attraction; it is not really my intent to prove the scientific basis of the Law of

Attraction. The following **web page** gives some scientific explanation of the correlation between Quantum Physics and the *"like attracts like"* principle:

> *"Those who protest are totally right that like-charges repel each other in Quantum Physics – positive charges repel positive charges, for example – that's the electromagnetic force.*
>
> *But, there is another force that is 100 times stronger than the electromagnetic force, and physicists call that the "strong force" – it's the force that holds the nucleus of every atom together. The nucleus of an atom is composed of neutrons and positive-charged protons, which normally repel each other completely.*
>
> *Dr. Hideki Yukawa (Nobel prize in physics) discovered way back in 1935 (and it was confirmed in 1947 and accepted as fact ever since then), that neutrons and protons in the nucleus of the atom (together called nucleons) constantly emit "virtual particles" called "mesons" and that they exchange these mesons with another nucleon (proton) or with themselves, and this interaction is what creates the "strong force" that holds the nucleus of the atom (and therefore all of physical reality) together.*
>
> *In order to create this strong force, protons (nucleons) emit the virtual meson particles toward other like-particles in order to attract them into, or keep them in, the nucleus of an atom. The action and result that is created by this exchange of virtual particles among like-particles is that "strong force" itself – the strong force would not exist without this exchange of virtual particles.*

Thoughts are virtual particles. An atom, particles, everything that exists has intelligence and memory. Virtual particles are the thoughts of particles. Attraction would not exist without thoughts, the exchange of thoughts, and the exchange of virtual particles.

That's how like attracts like - by the exchange of information, virtual particles, thoughts – on the atomic level, and on the human interaction level. And, this attraction force is 100 times stronger than the repelling force.

Some say there can be no connection between the atomic level and thought, between particles and human interaction, that virtual particles cannot be thought, and that there is no proof for the **Law of Attraction** *in Quantum Physics.*

I did not make it up!! And this is not new information. A particle, whether it's a virtual particle or a real physical particle, does not even exist until an observer (i.e. a person) focuses a thought upon it and causes it to appear from nowhere. Before that moment, it was only a probability, a specific frequency, raw information that had no locality and no form. The act of a thought brought it into existence. And, raw information itself is a thought (intelligence), and a thought (intelligence) is raw information. ***These are all commonly accepted principles in Quantum Physics.***

The concept that a thought (human interaction) creates particles, that a thought creates physical form, has been put out in theory and later confirmed in research by many people. Among those theories are those of Max Planck in 1900 (quantum hypothesis), Niels Bohr in 1924 (probability waves), Werner Heisenberg in 1927, Richard

Feynman in 1949, J.S. Bell in 1964, David Bohm in 1970. There are many others, then and now.[ii] Einstein's research led to state that thoughts become things from a position of physics.[iii]

So this is not new information, the wealthy class have kept this secret for decades[iv]

Again, wrapping your brain around this is like eating an elephant. But Quantum Physics scientists agree across the board that *"like attracts like"* and that is good enough for me. As I explain the Biblical principles later on, you will see that the Word of God says the same thing.

We Are All Made up of Light

The first truth stated that all matter is made up of energy. Again, we have known for years through science that all matter is made up of atoms. We learned in middle school that atoms are made up of smaller particles in motion - photons, electrons, neutrons and quarks. Atoms are only a very small percentage of actual physical matter; the rest is just space (more than 99.99%). In actuality, we are only a small percentage of actual physical particles; the rest of us are just space. Quantum Physics tells us that light or electromagnetic energy holds together and makes up these particles. Therefore, all matter is actually some form of light or energy. You and I are made up of light. We are the LIGHT of the World.

We have a hard time accepting this principle because light is not dense. Light can shine through a window but we cannot walk through a window. This has to do with the density of atoms in a molecule or the space between atoms and the rate at which they vibrate. This gives the illusion of solids, liquids or gases.

The Human Body Gives off Frequencies

Because, like everything else, we are made up of waves of energy, then, like everything else, we vibrate and give off a frequency.

> *"According to Dr. Robert O. Becker in his book, The Body Electric, the human body has an electrical frequency and that much about a person's health can be determined by it. Frequency is the measurable rate of electrical energy flow that is constant between any two points. Everything has frequency."*

> *"Dr. Royal R. Rife found that every disease has a frequency. He has found that certain frequencies can prevent the development of disease and that others would destroy diseases. Substances of higher frequency will destroy diseases of lower frequency.*

> *"In 1992, Bruce Taino of Taino Technology, an independent division of Eastern State University in Cheny, Washington, built the first frequency monitor in the world. Taino has determined that the average frequency of a healthy human body during the daytime is 62 to 68 Hz. When the frequency drops, the immune system is*

compromised. If the frequency drops to 58 Hz, cold and flu symptoms appear; at 55 Hz, diseases like Candida take hold; at 52 Hz, Epstein Bar and at 42 Hz, Cancer. Taino's machine was certified as 100 percent accurate and is currently being used in the agricultural field today."

*"The study of frequencies raises an important question concerning the frequencies of substances we eat, breathe, and absorb. Many pollutants have low frequencies and cause the body's healthy frequencies to be lowered and weakened. Processed or canned food has a frequency of zero and tends to lower healthy frequencies within the body towards degenerative diseases. Fresh produce has up to 15 Hz; dry herbs from 12 to 22 Hz; and fresh herbs from 20 to 27 Hz. Essential oil frequencies start at 52 Hz and go as high as 320 Hz; which is the frequency of Rose Oil. **These higher frequencies create an environment in which disease, bacteria, virus, fungus, cancer, etc., CANNOT live...**[v]*

Studies show that positive emotions create higher Hz or wavelength frequencies while negative emotions give off lower Hz. By the same notion, thoughts and intent have the same effect. Negative thoughts produce lower Hz than positive thoughts. There is a great deal of scientific evidence in the past few years validating these findings and the evidence can be easily researched. Muscle testing is a technique which determines a positive or negative flux of frequency. Lie detector tests are based on this energy theory also. Muscle testing has now been validated after millions of independent studies to verify its validity and reliability. Persons in a positive emotional state or thinking positive thoughts registered much higher on a strength scale than persons in a negative state.

In the book, *Power vs. Force*[vi], Dr. David Hawkins goes into great detail about the implications. This book also explores in detail the vibration of different situations and environments.

Have you ever entered a room and just felt bad? You were probably picking up a low frequency. Demonic or evil situations give off a low frequency. The anointing gives off a high frequency. I believe the presence of angels gives off a really high frequency also. The implications of this in a healing environment are that releasing negative trapped emotions results in a higher overall frequency and the ability to choose to think more positive thoughts and change the unconscious negative belief systems. You can learn more about the integration of inner healing and releasing trapped emotions at my personal website,

"IntegratedLifestrategies.com" and about the work of Dr. Bradley Nelson, the developer of Emotion Code Therapy at "Healerslibrary.com." Trapped emotion work is based on principles of Quantum Physics; it is not based on any particular spiritual beliefs. I have incorporated it into my practice and have seen great results.

It has become recognized in the medical profession as a proven fact that physical health is directly related to thought life and emotions and that more than 80% of all illness is related to emotional and mental stress. There are many books on this topic. The allopathic medical model acknowledges this truth but it still focuses only on treating symptoms and not identifying roots.

Experiments of Dr. Masaru Emoto

In the past few years, the experiments of Dr. Masaru Emoto have gained much acclaim. Dr. Emoto took water samples from a polluted river in Japan and subjected them to different treatments. He subjected some to classical music, some to heavy metal music, some to prayers, some to negative critical words and some to positive encouraging words. On some samples, he taped words on the vial that held the water but nothing was spoken (no sound waves, just thoughts). After an equal period of time, he quick froze the water and cut samples from the ice to place under a microscope. The resulting pictures are below[vii].

The outcome of this experiment demonstrated that positive thoughts, words and emotions affected the molecular structure of water in a beautiful, structured way and that negative thoughts, words and emotions affected the same water samples in a destructive way. Humans are more than 60% water. The point is that our words and what we listen to impact our very cells and DNA. Stop for a minute and think about everything you have said and thought about today; what kind of water crystals were you creating? Even more surreal and scary is the proof that thoughts, feelings and emotions have a definite physical impact on our bodies as well. Most medical experts will agree now that the cause of most diseases is rooted in emotions and negative belief systems.

So the human body is made up of energy that gives off a frequency or wavelength. Our thoughts, feelings, emotions on both a conscious and unconscious level create harmony or chaos within our body and also give off a correlating vibration or wavelength that extends outside of us. Sounds, music, foods, smells, and other people generate frequencies that directly affect ours. Disease can only exist in a low vibration environment. This paradigm is now proven from many scientific sources. Does this information make you hungry to know more about this?

Before   After

Effect on Water of
Immune Vibration

500 people sending
positive thoughts
to bottled water

Prayer over Water

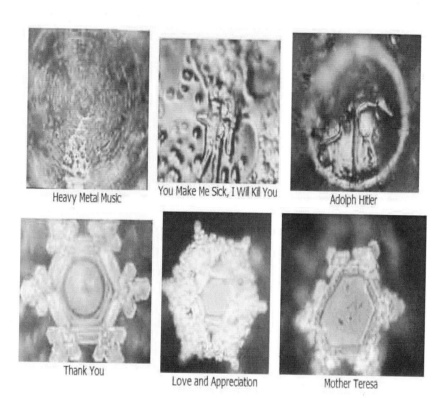

Heavy Metal Music

You Make Me Sick, I Will Kill You

Adolph Hitler

Thank You

Love and Appreciation

Mother Teresa

CHAPTER 2

THE LAW OF ATTRACTION AND *THE SECRET*

Given this established paradigm, the next principle (Truth #3 from Chapter 1) of Quantum Physics is the foundational truth of the Law of Attraction. This can be easily understood with the words, "like attracts like." The frequency we emit has a certain wavelength. Positive emotions like love, joy, happiness, and gratitude have a high frequency or a short distance between the peaks of a wave. Positive thoughts and words give off the same positive frequencies. Harmonious melodies are high frequency wavelengths. Essential oils have recently been discovered to have effects on the body based on frequency theory. Rose oil, for example, has an incredibly high frequency of 320Hz. The opposite is true for negative emotions, thoughts, words, unnatural foods (like white refined sugar), pollution, chemicals, toxins etc.

As previously discussed, these waves attract using the Strong Force principle. High frequencies attract high frequencies and low frequencies attract low frequencies. In essence, love attracts love and hate attracts hate. The field of Attraction Coaching takes this principle in all of its many nuances and applications and helps people learn to change their lives by changing their thoughts and feelings. In the book, *The Secret*[viii], Rhonda Byrne compiles lists of principles from successful attraction coaches and teachers.

Summary of *The Secret*

The Law of Attraction was made popular by Rhonda Byrne in the 2006 book, *The Secret* and was quickly made into a video that sold very successfully. At that time, information about the Laws of Quantum Physics had not become as mainstream or easily accessible as in recent years. Readers of *The Secret* looked at these principles from a strictly metaphysical stance and while many embraced them, a large majority of both Christians and non-Christians alike wrote this principle off as a New Age metaphysical principle. *The Secret* is considered by many as a text manual for The Law of Attraction. The bullet points below highlight much of its application of the Law of Attraction.

- Like attracts like, in word, emotion and thought

- Thoughts become things. We can attract and create

- We "order" what we want with our thoughts. If we do this deliberately then we can expect our desires to manifest.

- People think about what they don't want, which attracts that to them

- The universe was made from a thought

- Thoughts are always planting seeds

- Feelings let us know what we are thinking

- We can make a choice to change our thoughts and then deliberately add emotions to them

- If we think love, we will get love back etc.

- Believe that the universe is for you and then have faith

- When you try to figure out how what you want is going to manifest then you emit doubt.

- The practice of Law of Attraction is feeling what it is like to have it all now.

- Attracting may require action but it will be joyful to do it.

- Every possibility for your life already exists right now, Time is a construct and does not really exist and doubt keeps what we want from manifesting

- Size doesn't matter, it is as easy for the universe to produce a million dollars as a dollar

- Ask, Believe, Receive

- Practice gratitude

- Expect what you want

- Visualize. There is no difference in the brain between actual experience and visualizing an experience

- Giving joyfully feels good and creates attraction. Giving Sacrificially is operating in lack

- Think abundance. Don't say things like – "I can't afford it"

- Abundance is not just money – it is in all areas and includes inner peace

- Law of Attraction includes thoughts about oneself

- Disease and sickness are a by-product of how you think about yourself

- Words and thoughts create your world. If you use the word "battle," then expect a battle

- What we resist persists. (Carl Jung) We focus attention on negative things and it expands

- We determine our destiny based on our perspective about it.

There are other, more specific points in *The Secret* as well. These are the key ones detailed. Each chapter gives examples of people using the Law of Attraction in their lives.

While the allusion is not made, it turns out the title word, "secret" is the same reference that, according to Kevin Trudeau in his tape series, "You wish is your command"[ix], has been used for decades by the very rich on how they kept making money. He explains that when Napoleon Hill wrote *Think and Grow Rich,*[x] Henry Ford did everything in his power to keep the book from getting out int the general market. According to Trudeau, the very rich wanted this principle to be kept a "secret." It was their own "genie in a bottle" and from what he says, the rich really know how to work this principle consistently. So the billionaires in this world have all learned this from each other and become richer. Trudeau also states that the wealthy believe that you are born to be wealthy, so sharing this principle with the not-wealthy would not matter because they are not entitled to wealth. (He made this as a general statement). I find that very fascinating. It seems that secret societies of people have been making application of "As a man Thinketh"[xi] from Psalms 23:7 without knowing the God who wrote that scripture. That sounds like faith to me. They have faith in a principle but not in a person. Does this concept make you feel uncomfortable? Does it seem wrong to believe in good things happening to you or wishing for your heart's desires without "delighting in the Lord?" (**Psalm 37:4**) This was one of the problems that the church (in general) had with the book, *The Secret.* The next chapter suggests other conflicts.

I believe that with the rapidly spreading teaching on Quantum Physics, that perhaps 'the secret' was destined to 'get out' and then those that have guarded this for decades decided to be involved in the release of this information. I pray that the next few chapters will bring some understanding of the laws of the universe and how I believe God wants us to understand and apply them.

CHAPTER 3

THE CHRISTIAN CHURCH'S CONFLICTS WITH *THE SECRET'S* CONTENT

The "name it and claim it" theology and practice from the "Word of Faith" movement experienced a peak in the early nineties. After the exposure of corruption and deception by well-known TV evangelists who promoted this theology, many Christians were left with a bad taste in their mouths for the principles espoused. Instead of seeing the whole picture of true abundance and prosperity that the Bible suggests, the immature application of faith suggests that we simply ask for cars, money and furs and they will appear. These televangelists took advantage of this "magical" principle by promising wealth to those who sent money, while they were exploiting the wealth deceptively. In knee-jerk reaction, many people "threw the baby out with the bath water" and, in their hearts, vowed that wealth was evil. There is much debate theologically on wealth and though that is not the purpose of this book, scripture points to the state of the **condition of the heart** as a central issue in regard to wealth. No thing, in and of itself, is inherently evil, only what we do with it. Wealth is a necessary tool for the spread of the gospel and ministry across the world and it can also be an idol and bondage. It depends on how it is viewed by the person. Is it an idol? Does it require corruption to maintain or produce? Proverbs and other scripture repeatedly tell us that poverty is undesirable and a curse. But in scripture, wealth is also discussed with great caution. Again, my point is not to debate theology but only to share my observations.

I believe that when *The Secret* emerged, especially in video form, it sounded much like the "name it claim it" gospel that didn't include a relationship with Jesus. This was my initial response to seeing the video. I thought, "This is just about greed and materialism." I believe that the principles of Quantum Physics and the Bible reciprocally support each other and that is the purpose of my book. However, every truth can be mistaught and abused and the religionists and theologians love to extol their intellectual arguments to dismantle truth. I am not defending the book, *The Secret,* only again pointing out the Christian Church's tendency to "throw the baby out with the bathwater."

I believe the bottom line is God wants us to live and prosper however that is defined; the Bible supports this, and depicts poverty as a curse. **The problem is always a heart issue, not a wealth issue**. The Kingdom of God requires money to expand. Running from wealth because of a fear of corruption will probably ensure you stay poor. Looking to

God for a pure heart about wealth is a far better solution than poverty.

1 John 2:15 says:

"15 Do not love the world or anything in the world. If anyone loves the world, love for the Father[a] is not in them. 16 For everything in the world—the lust of the flesh, the lust of the eyes, and the pride of life—comes not from the Father but from the world. 17 The world and its desires pass away, but whoever does the will of God lives forever."

God does not want us to lust after worldly things, but, once again, factions of the Church want to throw the baby out with the bathwater. Wealth is about stewardship of God's finances for the Kingdom not about hedonistic pleasures or seeking happiness in material possessions. Perhaps having wealth lends itself to greater temptation but poverty is definitely seen as a curse.

Having established this thought, the problem many had with *The Secret* is similar to the "name it and claim it" theology. Because the author was not a professing Christian, it was inclusive to the whole world, not just Christian believers. It does not state the existence of a God who is the Creator, but talks about an anonymous universe that is for us only because we believe it is for us, when in fact it is neutral. As you will see later, I believe God created the Laws of Attraction to govern the universe, but he gave us the outline of these laws in the Bible. Scripture tells us how the universe is governed, if we will listen and follow. This was not 'metaphysical'; it was written plainly long before the "self-help gurus" set foot on the earth. We do not look to the universe, we look to God. The principles of the *The Secret* are predominantly Biblical; it is just the lack of pointing towards the Creator of the Universe that can create disharmony with our spirit.

The Secret suggests our lives are blank slates and that we can potentially create multiple possibilities for ourselves. Christianity portrays a sovereign God who:

- Knew you from your mother's womb

   Psalm 139:13: *"For You did form my inward parts; You did knit me together in my mother's womb."*

   Jeremiah 1:4-5: *"The word of the LORD came to me saying, 5" Before I formed you in the womb I knew you, And before you were born I consecrated you; I have appointed you a prophet to the nations."...*

- Knows the number of hairs on your head

   Luke 12: 7: *"Indeed, the very hairs of your head are all numbered. Don't be afraid; you are worth more than many sparrows."*

- *H*as a destiny for you

> **Ephesians 1:5** - *"He **predestined** us for adoption to sonship through Jesus Christ, in accordance with his pleasure and Will."*

> **Jeremiah 29:11-13**: *"[11]For I know the plans I have for you," declares the LORD, "plans to prosper you and not to harm you, plans to give you hope and a future. [12] Then you will call on me and come and pray to me, and I will listen to you. [13] You will seek me and find me when you seek me with all your heart" (A specific word to Israel but showing God was involved in destiny)*

> **Romans: 28-31**: *"[28]And we know that in all things God works for the good of those who love him, who have been called according to his purpose. [29]For those God foreknew he also predestined to be conformed to the image of his Son, that he might be the firstborn among many brothers and sisters. [30]And those he predestined, he also called; those he called, he also justified; those he justified, he also glorified. [31]What, then, shall we say in response to these things? If God is for us, who can be against us?"*

Another reason that I believe *The Secret* was rejected by the Church was more because many people interpreted the video as being solely materialistic. The central theme of the gospel is that we *"lose our life to find it"* (**Matthew 10:39**); that we *"throw aside all weights" (which could include material things) and "run the race"* (**Hebrews 12:1***) and "run* *[your race] that you may lay hold [of the prize] and make it yours.*"(**1 Corinthians 9:24**) that we *deny himself [disown himself, forget, lose sight of himself and his own interests, refuse and give up himself] and take up his cross daily and follow Me*" (**Luke 9:23**) that we "die daily" (to self) (**1 Corinthians 15:31**); that we live our lives to hear Him say in Heaven, "*Well done my good and faithful servant*" (**Luke 19:17**) and that the body is not our home and at odds with being with the Lord. (**2 Corinthians 5:6**)

This all implies that we should not seek comfort or things for ourselves but everything is related to the gospel and making disciples. *The Secret* seemingly comes across with the message that having everything we think we want will make us happy. The Bible suggests that true "happiness" which we would translate "peace and joy," comes from surrendering our will to Jesus, and seeking relationship with Him as the primary, truly authentic source of happiness, forsaking all else.

I would suggest too that one of the issues many Christians may have had with *The Secret* was the thought, "Surely it can't be this easy." There is always this underlying voice of our flesh that we have to work hard for everything, even our relationship with the Lord. We easily miss the grace part of the gospel because religion and the model of the world would constantly remind us that performance is necessary. The people successful in Law of Attraction work have a simple faith that this principle is the governing structure of the Universe and that they simply have to apply the principle. They divorce it from an existing God who governs the Law of Attraction. Ultimately they separate the principle from any kind of relationship. Most of us in the body of Christ have significant father wounds from our childhood. Thus believing the God of the universe loves us and wants to give us the desires of our heart triggers painful unconscious memories of an earthly father who was not like this loving God. It offends us to think that the universe is like a vending machine and yet the Law of Attraction suggests a slightly more complex version of this.

The Secret book does elaborate more than the video. It does talk about having "stuff" but ultimately it points to an inner peace as the source of true happiness. The thought that having everything we want seems hedonistic to a Christian; but then many Christians spend their lives scrambling just to survive and never get to peace and joy because they have not been able to experience the scriptures just mentioned. There are many reasons why they cannot get to peace and joy; it is not a simple task. As you continue to read, I believe you will be enlightened about exactly where the Law of Attraction fits into God's big scheme of things and how to use it in your life in a way that aligns with God's Heart and His Word.

Recently, Billy Graham made the statement that "He wished he had spent more time alone with God and less time doing ministry." Wow! Can you imagine being the single most successful minister of this century, a household name, not having any need for material things, having successful and fulfilling relationships and making this statement? This reveals a deep truth that our greatest place of peace and joy comes from intimacy with the Holy Spirit.

The Law of Grace and the Science of Chaos

The Secret does not take into account the Law of Grace and Mercy. The Law of Gravity applies most of the time to us humans. Rarely can someone jump off a five-story building and not splat onto the ground. I don't suggest you try it. Peter walked on water but I haven't yet met someone who has truly done this successfully. The Law of Aerodynamics and Lift trumps the Law of Gravity so airplanes and birds can fly. Chapter five will discuss the hierarchies in laws more in depth. *The Secret* does not suggest there are hierarchies, The Bible does.

There is a principle in meteorology called "The Science of Chaos." This principle suggests that the laws of weather are so intertwined; they cannot truly be accurately predicted. It refers to the "butterfly effect" meaning that the flight pattern of a butterfly in Rio de Janeiro could affect the weather in New York City. The whole world affects every other part so intricately (Quantum Physics includes this in the Law of Entanglement) that meteorologists can never be 100% accurate in forecasting weather because they cannot factor in all of the variables accurately. I believe that God's operations in the world are similar to this law. His complexity is far beyond our complete understanding and sometimes He trumps the Law of Gravity, like he did when Peter stepped out of the boat. *The Secret* does not allow for this idea that a supernatural God might trump the Law of Attraction. Testimonies affirm that sometimes God just seems to override it. *The Secret* might agree that your faith (Like Peter's) could cause you to override the Law of Gravity, but that explanation would not explain why Shadrach, Meshach and Abednego did not burn when cast into the fiery furnace. The hand of God can and does transcend the other laws. He is involved, and perhaps if we were smarter, we could discover that all of His actions were governed by laws, but supernatural stories throughout history suggest that He does not always stay within the guidelines that He set forth for the Universe to operate. It is man's nature to try to order his world and create rules and boxes to make himself feel safe. *The Secret* gives pat formulas for all operations. Exceptions suggest that there are more complex rules than just these. *The Secret* would suggest that if something doesn't manifest, you either didn't really want it or you were conflicted in your unconscious. This makes exceptions easy to explain. Supernatural occurrences might suggest that the Law of Attraction is not including God's direct intervention or that the Science of Chaos might be involved. I would posit that the prayers of other people are a key factor in the Science of Chaos. We are all connected.

So while the Quantum Physics principle of the Law of Attraction has truth to it, in how we live our lives (as will be discussed in the next chapters), the neat package suggested by *The Secret*, negates a personal God who may sovereignly move undeservedly in mysterious ways in a person's life to display His glory. He may have created the Law of Attraction to govern the universe but He still remains and wants us to remember that He is God and above all of His creation.

As I listen to tapes and read Law of Attraction books, I am intrigued by this concept that we create our own destiny. As you will read, I support this idea with scriptural and spiritual laws. However, what makes my life so incredible is that I have a personal relationship with a real and living God. His presence has no words to compare; it is unlike any other sensation. The connection I feel with the Holy Spirit in any given moment when I pay attention makes all of the stuff and success of this world pale in comparison. The Law of Attraction cannot counterfeit this and it truly is ours for the asking. We have to seek and desire it like everything else. We have to believe it is real, although the Holy Spirit apprehends many who don't believe in Him prior to this apprehension. So perhaps, we as Christians, can have the best of both worlds; a powerful relationship with Jesus Christ, the Father and the Holy Spirit and the understanding of how to manifest a kingdom destiny of good fruit using principles of attraction.

CHAPTER 4

SCRIPTURES SUPPORTING THE LAW OF ATTRACTION

A s I proposed earlier, what if God created the Law of Attraction to essentially govern the universe? Everything He does has an order to it; we observe this in nature and science all the time. What if the theory of the Law of Attraction is not a different, New Age or metaphysical theory? What if it is completely supported by scripture? What if God's design was for the universe to fundamentally run by this law?

Quantum Physics principles translate to a few key premises. They can be understood in the following statements.

- Overall...Like attracts like
- You attract what you think and say
- You get what you give/reap what you sow
- You create your own world with what you believe in your head and in your heart
- Whatever you focus attention on/give energy to grows and/or manifests.

"As a Man thinks in his heart, so is he"....**Proverbs 23:7**
*"Do not conform to the pattern of this world, **but be transformed** by the renewing of your mind..."* **Romans 12:2**

The experiments of Dr. Emoto showed the effects of thinking on molecules of water. Remember that he did different experiments; some with music, some with words spoken and some with words written (intention/thought). Medical Science has confirmed that more than 80% of disease is rooted in problems in the unconscious belief systems. If we are only conscious of about 15% of the 60,000+ thoughts we think every day, then our life is guided by that unconscious. (I will use this word synonymously with the word "heart." This aligns with the Law of Attraction. If our past is wrought with trauma, abuse and pain, our unconscious belief systems about ourselves will be dominated by self hate, low self-esteem, bitterness, resentment, blame, self-pity, jealousy, anger, fear and other forms of these emotions. If "like attracts like," we will become what we think.

Matthew 9.29 says: (Amplified Bible)

"Then he touched their eyes, saying, 'According to your faith, (and trust and reliance on the power in me) be it done to you,'"

Matthew 21:21 says: (Amplified Bible) says:
"And Jesus answered them, 'Truly I say to you, if you have faith (a firm relying trust) and do not doubt, you will not only do what has been done to the fig tree, but even if you say to this mountain, be taken up and cast into the sea, it will be done'."

Apparently God feels this bears repeating. **Mark 11:23** says:

*"Truly I say to you, whoever says to this mountain, be lifted up and thrown into the sea and does not doubt at all in his **heart**, but believes that what he says will take place, it will be done for him."*

The word "believe" is found in the Book of John 83 times (in the Amplified Bible).

John 14:1 says: (Amplified Bible)
"Do not let your hearts be troubled, distressed, agitated. You believe (in and adhere to and trust in and rely) on God; believe (in and adhere to and trust in and rely) also on Me."

Matthew 8:13 says:
"Then to the centurion Jesus said, Go; it shall be done for you as you have believed. And the servant boy was restored to health at that very moment."

Often I have seen the church limit the concept of believing to the gospel – believing that Jesus is God and died for our sins. But Jesus is talking about so much more of what his sacrifice actually means for us.

The word "believe" consistently contains these three meanings – "rely, trust, and adhere to." We call this "faith" but it also implicates our thought life in every conscious and unconscious detail. Jesus repeatedly links belief with the impossible. He connects faith with seeing those things manifest. He says many times that in order for it to manifest, we must not doubt.

James 1:5-8 says,
[5]"If any of you lacks wisdom, you should ask God, who gives generously to all without finding fault, and it will be given to you. [6]But when you ask, you must believe and not doubt, because the one who doubts is like a wave of the sea, blown and tossed by the wind. [7]That person should not expect to receive anything from the Lord. [8]Such a person is double-minded and unstable in all they do.

Whatever we have belief in/have faith for/focus our attention on, we empower and it grows. Jesus repeatedly told us to have faith – to believe. Faith vibrates very high and thus attracts good things. Like attracts like. James clearly states that if we doubt that God gives generously and does it without finding fault (like we think we have to earn it), then we walk in doubt and should not expect to receive it. In other words, it isn't because God doesn't want us to have what we desire. He says clearly in **Psalms 37:4**, "Delight yourself in the Lord and He will give you the desires of your heart;" but we doubt his goodness and we don't "trust, rely, adhere to." this attribute about Him. Doubt and fear do not vibrate high and don't attract good things. When we sow faith, we move mountains, when we sow doubt we don't. Fear, worry, and doubt vibrate very low and attract like things.

I was always puzzled by the scripture in **Matthew 25:29**, "*[29] For to everyone who has will more be given, and he will be [ ]furnished richly so that he will have an abundance; but from the one who does not have, even what he does have will be taken away."* *(Amplified)* I never really heard a satisfactory explanation of what Jesus was talking about. What if Jesus is referring to the Law of Attraction? Those who "have" have understood and have asked, sought and knocked and kept a high vibration to keep attracting more good things. Those who are in lack have kept a low vibration, state of worry and lack of faith. If they continue to doubt and vibrate low, they will continue to lose what they do have. God is no respecter of persons. He gives us the guideline to live a life of peace and joy if we will choose to follow the blueprint. Pause and review your life for a few minutes applying this concept and see if you see any patterns where your beliefs about things, yourself, others, God and/or the universe have been reinforced in your experience but not in the lives of others.

Matthew 6:25-31 says: *"Don't worry about food, clothes, drink etc. [26] look at the birds of the air, they neither sow nor reap nor gather into barns, and yet your heavenly father keeps feeding them. Are you not worth much more than they? [27] And who of you by working and being anxious can add one unit of measure to his stature or to the span of his life? [28] Consider the lilies of the field and learn thoroughly how they grow; they neither toil nor spin. [29] yet I tell you, even Solomon. in all of his magnificence was not arrayed like one of these (1Kings 10:4-7) [30] ..But if God so clothes the grass of the field, which today is alive and green and tomorrow is tossed into the furnace, will He not much more surely clothe you, you of little faith? [31] ...Therefore, do not worry ...your heavenly Father knows well that you need them all."*

God clearly says that He (not the universe) knows your needs. He also makes it clear that being a Christian believer is not a prerequisite for Him meeting your needs. Jesus was speaking to the masses not just his followers. He was making a statement about the character of God. But He does directly correlate this with not worrying. I am not going to get into discussions like people starving all over the world and how that seemingly contradicts this scripture. This scripture illustrates the principal of getting what we believe, think or expect. It illustrates the concept that God is for us and will take care of our needs.

Then Jesus says in **Matthew 6:33:**

> *"But seek first of all **His kingdom** (New King James says, "The Kingdom of God") and his righteousness and then all these things taken together will be given you."*

"All these things" is a reference to the scripture I just quoted. They are food, drink, and other provision. Jesus is saying if we will seek the Kingdom of God first, then all of our needs will be met; rather than spend our time and energy worrying about getting our needs met ourselves. So, what is **"The Kingdom of God"?** One of the most impactful revelations to me about this came from the teaching of Dr. George Burriss, II Ph.D.[xii]

This definition is given in **Romans 14:17-18,**

> *"After all the Kingdom of God is not a matter of food and drink, but is **righteousness, peace and joy** in the Holy Spirit. Because anyone who serves Christ in this way is pleasing to God and receives human approval."*

So:

- If we seek these three things,

- **righteousness,** (Jesus is our righteousness because ours is as *"filthy rags"* **(Isa 64:6)**,

- **peace** and **joy** in the Holy Spirit (our trust, reliance and relationship with Jesus) then

- We will have all that we need. ("all these things")

- If we seek after our needs, then we are operating in doubt and worry. (And are double-minded according to James)

- Peace and joy vibrate high. Worry vibrates low.

- When we vibrate high, we please God. (Because that is faith)

- When we vibrate high we have man's favor (attract good things)

Like attracts like.

Did you know that in the advent of brain science, it has been discovered that the brain is wired for peace and joy? Dr. Alan Schore has done extensive research on the physiology of the brain and written on this topic.[xiii] E. James Wilder, et al has simplified these very complicated books to explain that **God wired our brains for peace and joy.**[xiv] Everything we do is motivated by our brain's attempts to return to a state of peace or joy. Babies need their secure attachments to bring them from a state of distress back to peace and joy. This is crucial in the brain's ability to later on be able to return to states of peace and joy. Addictions, compulsions and everything we do is motivated by a drive to return to this state. Freud called this "the pleasure principle." It has often been misunderstood by critics to say that Freud believed that we are driven by pleasure as in how we define "hedonism." But we are driven by our belief systems. If worry allows us to feel in control, then that brings a degree of peace to our mind. But fear and worry lead to attracting low vibration or negative things. Authentic joy and peace that come from trusting in the Lord for everything vibrate high and attract high vibration or good things. Trust is a scary thing because it must be rooted in a deep knowing that we are loved.

1 John 5:14-15 says:

> [14] *"This is the confidence we have in approaching God: that if we ask anything according to His will, He hears us.* [15] *And if we know that He hears us—whatever we ask—we know that we have what we asked of Him."*

We know God wants to give us the desires of our heart (thus this is His will). If we are delighting in Him then we can believe that our heart's desires will align with what is good for our lives (at least in general); and if we don't doubt (**James 1**) then our desires will manifest. This defines exactly what the Law of Attraction says in principle. The question becomes, "What do we truly desire?"

The challenge in living truly is more about how to actually execute living a life of peace and joy which I will address in subsequent chapters.

Another revelation from Dr. George Burriss came regarding what The Bible actually defines as God's will in **Ephesians 5:17-20**:

> 17"*Therefore do not be foolish, but understand what the Lord's will is. 18 Do not get drunk on wine, which leads to debauchery. Instead, be filled with the Spirit, 19 speaking to one another with psalms, hymns, and songs from the Spirit. Sing and make music from your heart to the Lord, 20 always giving thanks to God the Father for everything, in the name of our Lord Jesus Christ.*"

God's will is:
1. Don't seek after hedonistic pleasures (debauchery)
2. Be filled with the Spirit instead of the world (seek to sow to the spirit and not the flesh)
3. Edify and encourage each other, affirm and do not criticize each other.
4. Worship the Lord in our heart
5. Live in a state of gratitude to the Lord

All of these things are high vibration states of existence. God's will is that we stay at peace and joy, this is the Kingdom. This is different from destiny (callings, anointing and spheres of influence)

So how do we do this? It seems like an impossible task. The world is full of pain, evil, stress, sickness, hunger etc. We are bombarded every day with negative events that give us the message that life is cruel and the universe is against us. We are continually fed the message that the way to solve the world's problems is to worry. Joy and peace seem like they can only belong to the heartless, cold and self-centered human beings who don't care about the rest of the world.

Philippians 4:6-8 gives us the simple answer:

> [6] *"Do not be anxious about anything, but in every situation, by prayer and petition, with thanksgiving, present your requests to God.* [7] *And the peace of God, which transcends all understanding, will guard your hearts and your minds in Christ Jesus. (Remember, don't doubt, "believe," don't worry)* [8] *Finally, brothers and sisters, whatever is true, whatever is noble, whatever is right, whatever is pure, whatever is lovely, whatever is admirable—if anything is excellent or praiseworthy—think about such things "*

Paul is saying something incredible. He is telling us not to think about anything negative. He is saying God wants us to focus only on positive things, period. We would call that having a "Pollyanna" outlook. But in effect, the Law of Attraction principles and the scriptures just discussed are saying this very thing. Whatever we focus on is what we empower and impacts our body, soul and spirit. Staying at a place of peace and joy requires we deliberately choose to focus on positive things when we are in control of what we think. Remember Dr. Emoto's water experiments.

In my experience, few people have really experienced peace. In our busy and complex world, there is much to worry about. This is the mantra of most people. Peace requires a deliberate seeking out. Do you seek out peace? Some people confuse peace with boredom. Some people feel useless when they are at peace because busyness equals self- worth.

The Law of Reciprocity vs. the Law of Sowing and Reaping

In the Law of Attraction, an elaboration of this principle includes the idea of reciprocity. In basic terms, we get what we give. We give love and get love in return. We give greed and selfishness; we get greed and selfishness in return. This is the Law of Reciprocity.

The word "karma" has become a household word. It is used in Hindu, and other religious philosophies.[xv] It refers to life's lessons which determine future lives. Since Christianity does not embrace reincarnation, the household understanding of Karma is the idea of cause and effect. It means that whatever we do sets action in motion and there is a consequence to us. In its basic, everyday application; if you help the old lady walk across the street, something good will happen to you. In the Bible, we see the concept of Sowing and Reaping.

Galatians 6:7-10 says,

⁷ Do not be deceived: God cannot be mocked. A man reaps what he sows. ⁸ Whoever sows to please their flesh, from the flesh will reap destruction; whoever sows to please the Spirit, from the Spirit will reap eternal life.⁹ Let us not become weary in doing good, for at the proper time we will reap a harvest if we do not give up.¹⁰ Therefore, as we have opportunity, let us do good to all people, especially to those who belong to the family of believers."

This passage is saying a great deal about the spiritual principles that govern the universe and what most people think of as "karma." The Law of Attraction is all about sowing and reaping because "Like Attracts Like." There are many scriptures where this principle is even further detailed. In **Matthew 13,** Jesus gives the parable of the *farmer sowing seeds, the parable of the mustard seed and yeast:*

²³ But the seed falling on good soil refers to someone who hears the word and understands it. This is the one who produces a crop, yielding a hundred, sixty or thirty times what was sown."

³¹ He told them another parable: *"The kingdom of heaven is like a mustard seed, which a man took and planted in his field.³² Though it is the smallest of all seeds, yet when it grows, it is the largest of garden plants and becomes a tree, so that the birds come and perch in its branches."*

³³ He told them still another parable: "The kingdom of heaven is like yeast that a woman took and mixed into about sixty pounds^[b] of flour until it worked all through the dough."

Jesus gives metaphors of the concept of multiplication. When we sow, what we reap is much greater. In the Law of Expansion, what we give energy to we empower and it grows;

we get back what we give multiplied. A small amount of yeast allows a lot of dough to expand. It is interesting that Jesus also talks about bad yeast (the Pharisees) *(Matt 16:5-12)*. So the law of expansion works in the negative too.

Luke 6:38 says: (the Expanded Bible)
[38] Give, and ·you will receive [[L] it will be given to you]. You will be given much [[L] ...a good Luke 6:38 measure...]. ·Pressed down [Compacted], shaken together, and running over, it will spill into your lap [[C] the image is of grain overflowing its container]. The ·way you give to [standard/measure you use with] others is the ·way God will give to [standard/measure God will use with] you."

Jesus has just said that what you reap will be expanded from what you sow. Perhaps Jesus is talking about the manner in which you give or the state of your heart when; that this is how it returns to you. The Law of Attraction focuses on your thoughts or intentions. So you could give with bad intention (reluctantly) and not have the same result as giving with good intention. We can give in order to get and the principle still works; but I believe the greater multiplication happens when we give to give because the vibration is higher. When we give out of love, we attract a greater return than giving out of law.

2 Corinthians 9:7 says: (Amplified)
[7] Let each one [give] as he has made up his own mind and purposed in his heart, not reluctantly or sorrowfully or under compulsion, for God loves (He takes pleasure in, prizes above other things, and is unwilling to abandon or to do without) a cheerful (joyous, "prompt to do it") giver [whose heart is in his giving].

Malachi 3:10 says:

*"Bring all the tithes (the whole tenth of your **in**come) **in**to the storehouse, that there may be food **in** my house, and prove **Me** now by it', says the Lord of hosts, if I will not open the windows of heaven for you and pour you out a blessing, that there shall not be room enough to receive it."*

This principle applies to giving in general, not just money. There are principles about first fruits and the tithe that fall under God's laws. The point is about having the intention to bless God/bless others/bless God's Kingdom and do good. Remember that the harvest is always a multiplication of what was planted. The Law of Reciprocity says we should repay kindness for kindness or pay it forward. It says if we practice love (high vibration), and kindness (high vibration) we will attract the same. The Law of Sowing and Reaping, according to the Bible is better. It says that what we give will be supernaturally multiplied when it returns to us. This is about expansion. When we give with the intention of blessing God or the Kingdom of God, we in effect sow a mustard seed and the return is great. The Law of Expansion (A) combined with the Law of Reciprocity (B) equals the Law of Sowing and Reaping.(C) So A+B=C.

I love this example....Mary Elaine held a Bible Study in her home. Her family was going through a tough time financially but God allowed them to maintain their nice home. There were days when they didn't have enough food. Strangers came to the meetings in her home all the time. One day someone told her that God wanted them to give her some money and held out a wad of cash. Mary Elaine stuffed it in her pocket without counting it. She was thinking about the food they could buy for the five kids. A little while later, during the service, The Lord told Mary Elaine to give the wad of cash to a visiting missionary couple. She didn't even count the money but obediently handed them the cash **with great joy**. She knew to be obedient. Not long after that, someone pulled up into her driveway with a SUV loaded from top to bottom with food. She determined it was much more than the cash she had given away. In the same day, she demonstrated this principle. Over the years I have heard very many of these stories. You can never out-give God. I have seen and experienced this first hand.

The Law of Bitter Root Judgments

This Law is of Bitter Root Judgments is a subcategory of Sowing and Reaping. This is one of the fundamental principles developed by John and Paula Sandford of Elijah House International decades ago and has been implemented in prayer ministry for many thousands of people all over the world. I have found it to be consistently operating in people's lives according to its principles.

This principle is founded on **Matthew 7:1-5:**

[1] Do not judge and criticize and condemn others, so that you may not be judged and criticized and condemned yourselves. [2] For just as you judge and criticize and condemn others, you will be judged and criticized and condemned, and in accordance with the measure you [use to] deal out to others, it will be dealt out again to you. [3] Why do you [a] stare from without at the [b] very small particle that is in your brother's eye but do not become aware of and consider the beam [c] of timber that is in your own eye? [4] Or how can you say to your brother, Let me get the tiny particle out of your eye, when there is the beam [d] of timber in your own eye? [5] You hypocrite, first get the beam of timber out of your own eye, and then you will see clearly to take the tiny particle out of your brother's eye."

John Sandford developed the principle of "bitter root judgments." The Law of Bitter Root Judgments says that however you judge another person in your heart will be sent back to you and manifest in your own life. It may manifest by you directly experiencing the thing you judged or it may manifest in your spouse (because you are one with your spouse) He develops this principle using **Matthew 7:1-5, Galatians 6:7** and the command to honor our father and mother, **Exodus 20:12. Matthew 7:18** talks about a good tree cannot bear bad fruit and vice- versa. So seeds of judgment will produce bad trees in our life and we find the trees by seeing the bad fruit. Roots of bitterness defile others as described in **Hebrews 12:15**. This principle has been confirmed and used in ministry and inner healing for decades from training models such as Elijah House, Restoring the Foundations and Freedom and Fullness. Many thousands of people will verify that the areas in their life where they have judged others, especially their parents, have manifested the same experiences in their life as who they judged. Or they married someone who manifested the things they judged. "As a man thinks in his heart".....When we maintain constant thoughts that are judgmental or are critical about someone, we send out negative intentions into the universe. These are low vibration thoughts that will come back to us. **These judgments cause us to hold onto bitterness or resentment which become trapped and cause these persistent thoughts.** When we sow criticism, we reap criticism. When we sow bitterness, we reap bitterness. What we focus on, we empower and it expands in our life. When we curse someone, even in our hearts or thoughts, we send negative vibrations into the universe and that comes back to us. Bless and we are blessed; curse and we are cursed; forgive and we are forgiven; judge and we are judged; love and we are loved. The thing with God, though, is that it is always multiplied back to us. So if it is positive, it is multiplied positively and if it is negative, it is multiplied negatively.

Let me add a disclaimer that not everything bad that happens is because you made a judgment when you were a child. There are other causes in the universe for adversity; I am just focusing on Bitter Root Judgments.

There are many examples to give. I can remember God illustrating this to me one day when my husband lost his keys. He tended to misplace his keys every day. I remember thinking, "How can you do this every day? Why don't you just put them somewhere everyday where you know where they are?" (Which he later did) I was more irritated by the anger he displayed (towards himself) which triggered some of my own issues with anger. But I definitely judged him in my heart. That same day, I misplaced my keys in the house (which I hardly ever do) I remember laughing loudly as I realized that God was illustrating this principle to me clearly. I have spent the better part of 20 years making a concerted effort to become aware of my thoughts when I am judging. I make a point at the beginning or end of each day to review my thoughts and see whom I have judged, forgive them and repent. This principle is also illustrated in **Romans 2:2:**

Therefore you have no excuse or defense or justification, O man, whoever you are who judges and condemns another. For in posing as judge and passing sentence on another, you condemn yourself, because you who judge are habitually practicing the very same things [that you censure and denounce]."

I have noticed in my and most of the marriages of people I know, that the repeated arguments and conflicts almost always point back to childhood judgments both parties made of their parents (or siblings). They are then repeating the pattern of reaping and re-sowing judgments with the thoughts, "You are just like my _____ who also did _____ or was _____. This reciprocal reaping also illustrates the principle of "defilement." **Hebrews 12:15** says:

> [15]" See to it that no one falls short of the grace of God and that no bitter root grows up to cause trouble and defile many. "

What this means is that if we have judged in some area and carry that around, there is a pressure for other people to treat us in the manner we are reaping from the judgment. I have often seen this principle in action. I had a woman in a support group I was leading who was very sweet. However, she clearly had some kind of judgment regarding rejection. There was just something about her that made me want to reject her. I recognized it and fought hard to counteract this spiritual force. I would watch other people roll their eyes or look away in group when she was speaking. It was a very strong defilement with her. In terms of The Law of Attraction, on an unconscious level she expected rejection, rejected herself (because of the continual rejection) and attracted rejection (like attracts like). It created much heartache in me because it was an example of what I see so often; people have a **belief system** created out of (a) **painful event**(s) which then attracts the very thing to keep happening and reinforces the **"truth"** of this **belief system**. In her case it was, "no one likes me, everyone will reject me" Objectively speaking, she did nothing to deserve this, but it was pervasive in this group setting. In a marriage, couples continually defile each other in this manner, they attract what they expect. Often I hear couples say "they weren't like that before I married them" and truly this may be the case, because they were not reaping from the judgment until they "Became one" and there was defilement. If you think for a moment, I am sure you can find examples of defilement in your own life.

Different psychological theories all agree that we typically marry someone like our mom or dad because of unresolved conflict. Gestalt psychology calls this "unfinished business," other theories have coined the term "trauma bonding and trauma reenactment," but, statistically speaking, it is generally accepted in psychology of being true. The principle of defilement and bitter roots is a spiritual explanation for this. These principles say you will be drawn to the people who will cause you to reap the judgment sown and that you will defile each other.

Most Christians have many judgments stored against God as well. These judgments came from disappointments in relationship to parents (especially Dad) or interpretations of events that included God disappointing them. (God didn't show up) A common one is about not believing God really cares for me because something occurred somewhere and the only conclusion I could draw is that God wasn't paying attention and therefore my life doesn't really matter to Him.

Most people are not consciously aware that they are judging. It is done automatically. It is the way of the world. In general, we are easily offended and judge quickly. A judgment is usually identifiable because there is a thought like, "I would never do that." Imagine you are in a grocery store and you see a mom screaming at her child and you think, "What a mean mom, I would never do that." The next day you find yourself yelling at your own child inappropriately. This law has just been manifested. This also happens when we make a comparison. In comparing, we either judge the other person or we judge our self. Both conflict with **Philippians 4:8**. Maybe this seems impossible and is certainly challenging. The wonderful thing about the way God made us is that we get to repent and this stops the law in motion and negates it. Repentance means to 'change your mind" so when we repent of a judgment, we stop the intentions and get to change our vibration which changes the attraction.

Mark 11:24-25 *says:*
Therefore I tell you, whatever you ask for in prayer, believe that you have received it, and it will be yours.[25] And when you stand praying, if you hold anything against anyone, forgive them, so that your Father in heaven may forgive you your sins."

This illustrates the principle just explained. Holding something against someone is judgment. In **Matthew 18:21-35**, Jesus talks about *"The parable of the unforgiving servant"* In the parable, a king brings in a guy who owes him a million dollars and the guy begs for mercy. The king knows he will never be able to repay so he forgives him. The guy in turn hauls his friend into court for owing him ten dollars and the guy's friend begs for mercy. The main guy says "no way, throw him into (debtors) prison" The king hears about it and hauls in the unforgiving servant saying," Hey, I forgave you a million dollars and you won't forgive ten dollars? You blew it and now you'll be tormented in prison forever." While there are several interpretations of this; basically Jesus is saying that we will suffer if we don't forgive (be turned over to the tormentors) when we have been forgiven so very much by the king (Jesus/God). This is not about eternal salvation; this is about sowing and reaping. If we hold judgment and bitterness in and don't extend forgiveness and grace, then we will attract judgment in like manner. If we want grace, we sow grace, if we want to be criticized, we sow criticism. If we want God to answer prayer; which requires grace, then we release judgment and bitterness and sow grace. *Like attracts like.* Criticism, judgment, and bitterness vibrate low and don't attract good things. Forgiveness, grace and faith attract high and bring good things.

Do you know the technology behind noise-cancelling headphones? Basically the headphone sends out a frequency that is exactly opposite of the surrounding frequency and this cancels out the surrounding frequency, negating it and creating silence. Repenting and forgiving act on the same principle as noise cancelling headphones. In effect, they create a cancellation of the frequency. When we judge and are bitter, we send out a low-frequency wave. By forgiving and repenting of judgment, we cancel the frequency just sent and set ourselves up in a position to have a higher frequency. One example from my own life was going through a period where I felt rejected by my peers. I walked around vigilant for someone talking about me behind my back or a glance or look that communicated rejection. I did some healing work including forgiving all those people and repenting for judging people as being critical. (along with some healing in my low self-esteem that resulted from the rejection) Somehow, I stopped expecting rejection from other people and it stopped happening. I absolutely expect people to like me and accept me in general and that seems to me to be the experience I have with people. It never crosses my mind that anything is unlikable about me. If people seem to display that, then I let them have an opinion and my value is not undermined. I cancelled that out from occurring in my life. Do you see repeating patterns in your life? **Can you correlate these**

repeating patterns (bad fruit) to judgments you made at a younger age?

<hr>
Inner Vows
<hr>

Another one of Sandford's principles is about "inner vows." **We make vows along with judgments.** When someone hurts us, we judge them, ourselves, and/or God (or the universe) and out of fear we make vows. **Vowing is exerting our will to take control of our life.** If you think about us as sheep under the care of a shepherd. When something bad happens, we think that the shepherd is not caring for us (mom, dad, God etc.) so we leave the safety of the flock and decide to take care of our self in this area. This leads to an opening for fear, worry, and control and is the opposite of trust (relying on, adhering to) in God's desire for the best plan for our life. Because we don't realize that other factors have been the cause of the bad thing, we determine that God or the universe is not for us in this area. **Vows are unconscious determinations of "I will or I will never."** (And usually has an "I will do whatever it takes to ......") A common example I find is, "I will never be an alcoholic like my mother or father." (whatever it takes) Because this is rooted in fear and judgment, it creates a low vibration in this area and attracts the very thing we don't want to happen, thus reinforcing the untrue belief system the experience created in the first place. It is hard to recognize and acknowledge a lie when our experience has consistently reinforced a certain belief. An example is from a woman who had abuse issues in her life. She had vowed she would never let herself be abused again. Consistently she would be attracted to abusive people both male and female, in her life. When we cancelled the judgments about trusting people, being a victim, being protected and repented for the vow that she would never be abused again, her life improved greatly (we did some trapped emotion work and found other vows and judgments also). She started feeling safer and people started treating her with more respect. **Can you remember thinking in your heart at any point in your life "I will or I will never?"**

Blessing

If we take a step past negating bitter root judgments then we encounter the power of blessing. I highly recommend a current book by Kerry Kirkwood called, *The Power of Blessing.*[xvi] If repenting of judgment and forgiving have the effect of releasing us from the consequences of judgment per the Law of Bitter Root Judgments, then if we take our process one step further by blessing that person, we create a powerful vibration and sowing. The Hebrew word blessing is *barak* and in Greek is *eulogia.* It means, "To speak God's intention." When we bless, we, in effect, vibrate on God's frequency. **If**

our intention can change water molecules, then imagine what God's intention does!

James 3:5, 9-10 says:
⁵ Likewise, the tongue is a small part of the body, but it makes great boasts. Consider what a great forest is set on fire by a small spark.⁹ With the tongue we praise our Lord and Father, and with it we curse human beings, who have been made in God's likeness.¹⁰ Out of the same mouth come praise and cursing. My brothers and sisters, this should not be."

God's intention is to bless. We are made in His image. When we curse, we are not operating in our true identity and we create a negative vibration which attracts negative things to us. We undermine our given authority. We are making judgments. As we said, when we judge, we reap bad fruit back upon us whether it is in both word and thought/intention. When we repent, we negate. **But when we then bless, we sow God's intention and we reap a great reward for blessing.** Most of us have heard the definition of repentance. It means to change your mind. It isn't just saying sorry, it is changing what you think and intend. Blessing requires more than just our casual definition of repentance (to say sorry), it requires we move into a whole different space of love, joy, gratitude and/or peace. In order to bless, we actually have to think/intend something good towards the other person, not just act humbly about our own mistake. This is a new step that has a great effect in terms of attraction. So, you say, "How do I bless the guy who just raped my daughter?" I got it, not easy to do. But to bless could sound something like a prayer or declaration like, "I bless the life of this man so that God could use his crime to bring some kind of healing and transformation (to him or someone else). I bless that God could turn his story into a miraculous testimony. This is like declaring Romans **8:28**. Isn't this much more empowering? Having said that, there is recognition that some offenses are easier to let go of quickly than others, but the end result is that our response creates a ripple effect of impact either positively or negatively.

God said to Abraham in *Genesis 12:3*:

And I will bless those who bless you [who confer prosperity or happiness upon you] and [a]curse him who curses or uses insolent language toward you; in you will all the families and kindred of the earth be blessed [and by you they will bless themselves.

He was talking about the Jews. But are we not all God's children from the price Jesus paid? Are we not all "grafted into the vine" as believers? So this principle truly transfers to all men. Theological arguments will say that Jesus took on all our curses so that curses are not part of the New Covenant. So what if we substituted the concept of sowing and reaping in place of cursing. If you judge or curse someone, you will reap bad fruit.

You may say, "But what if someone is truly evil?" Well the Bible calls Satan, "The accuser of the Brethren" (**Revelations 12:10**) and we are to see evil as operating through someone because of demonic forces and not actually view the person as evil themselves. **Ephesians 6:12** says: *"We war not against flesh and* bl*ood, but against principalities, against powers, against the rulers of the darkness of this world."* It would be easier to separate the person from the evil spiritual force operating through them or deceiving them if we really thought that way. We all have flesh and the capacity for evil and all require God's grace and mercy. "There but for the grace of God, go I" (famous quote by John Bradford)," Satan's greatest delight is to separate brothers in Christ. He knows the power of unity. If he can keep us upset with one another, we lose the power of the Kingdom (remember, peace and joy). Staying offended guarantees that we keep our vibration low, reap bad fruit, miss blessings and God doesn't forgive our sins. Forgiving, repenting and blessing every situation that comes our way ensures that we stay at peace and joy, are in God's will, vibrate high, focus on good things, and create expansion by giving energy to positive things. I hate to say it, but I don't think what we have been doing has been working well (in general). Maybe it's time to try a different strategy to change the world. Look around at our current state and ask, "How's that working for us?"

Matthew chapter 7 ties these together also. The first verses in this chapter are about judging (as just quoted and taking the log out of our own eyes, (**v 4-5**). Immediately following this, Jesus says:

7 "Ask and it will be given to you; seek and you will find; knock and the door will be opened to you. 8 For everyone who asks receives; the one who seeks finds; and to the one who knocks, the door will be opened."

9 "Which of you, if your son asks for bread, will give him a stone? 10 Or if he asks for a fish, will give him a snake? 11 If you, then, though you are evil, know how to give good gifts to your children, how much more will your Father in heaven give good gifts to those who ask him! 12 So in everything, do to others what you would have them do to you, for this sums up the Law and the Prophets."

Once again we see this alignment about getting what we ask God for when we stay clean of bitter root judgments and when we bless (**v 12**) others. Maybe there is a direct correlation between judging/being critical of others and not seeing our prayers answered. Maybe when we live a life of not entertaining offense, we vibrate higher.

What is also interesting is to look at the verse in between the not judging and the asking parts of **Matthew 7**. **Matthew 7:6** says:

"Do not give dogs what is sacred; do not throw your pearls to pigs. If you do, they may trample them under their feet, and turn and tear you to pieces."

Not *throwing pearls to swine"* has generally been understood as not sharing things which are holy with people who don't understand them. In the context between **Matthew 7:1** and **Matthew 7:7,** I would like to suggest that this verse means to avoid people who don't get the principle of judgment and are highly judgmental, critical and gossip about others (we might call that a "religious spirit") and that hanging out with those people may cause us to judge them or others and, thus, we don't get the fruit of **Matthew 7:7.** Hanging out with gossipers is rarely a high vibration environment. If people don't receive the Law of Bitter Root Judgments, don't hang out with them, they might suck you in...

The Law of Attraction vs. Prayer

Have you ever thought about the difference between prayer and intention? We think that God only hears our prayers. We think that unless we address Him first, like "Dear God..." that He ignores the thoughts we have in our minds. Remember, if the water experiments had the same effect with intentions as words, then our thoughts about ourselves and others carry the same power as our words. This bears repeating. If you curse someone in your thoughts, you have cursed them in your words. If you bless them in your thoughts, you bless them with your words. **Intention carries the same weight as words.** The scripture in James says we should not bless and curse with the same tongue; do we do this in our thoughts?

One of the techniques to attract what you want using the Law of Attraction goes like this[xvii]:

1. You decide what you want (general or specific)

2. You think, feel, imagine and see that thing coming to pass. You have to have a burning desire for this thing to manifest. Your feelings are very important. Be very detailed. The brain cannot discern between real experience and visualization (same neurons fire under both conditions). You are creating a specific vibration for what you want to manifest. You want to focus on how having this will make you feel.

3. You repeat this exercise with the same intensity. You don't worry about the how it will come to pass and you don't demand a time frame.

4. When your belief lines up with your feelings (you know it will happen) then it will happen.

This is different from one of the authors of *The Secret* who says to just ask once and believe. The difference here I believe is that you have to keep doing the work until you really believe it will happen. This sounds very much like **Matthew 7:7** again:

Philippians 4:6 *(Amplified) says:*

"Do not fret or have any anxiety about anything, but in every circumstance and in everything, by prayer and petition ([a]definite requests), with thanksgiving, continue to make your

wants known to God." This is not so much a contradiction of keep asking but the idea is that you ask until you can let go of anxiety that it will be answered. This is the activation of faith."

We are constantly sowing every moment of every day, even in our silence. We spend time in deliberate prayer asking God to answer our requests, but then we negate our prayers, like noise-cancelling headphones by thinking negatively. If thoughts do indeed become things, then we pray negatively every time we dwell on negative things. Let's say my daughter occurs to me as being extremely strong-willed and stubborn and it occurs to me she is making bad choices in her life. If I am praying fervently she will listen to good advice and make better choices but my thoughts and words are declaring that she is making bad choices and very stubborn, then I am constantly negating my prayers with opposite frequencies. Does this ring true? Has this ever occurred to you? If we truly embraced the idea that every intention/thought we have is the same as a prayer, perhaps we would be more conscious of our thoughts. Remember Paul said, *"Pray without Ceasing"* **1 Thessalonians 5:17.** Perhaps Paul was making us aware that if there is no distinction between thoughts and prayer, then our thoughts need to be as deliberate as our prayers.

I remember before I knew about The Law of Attraction, I used to notice that God would answer my prayers but usually it was in some way I had not imagined. I would joke that when I prayed or asked God for something that I had to stop myself from thinking how He would bring it to pass just to save Him energy of having to create something I had not thought of. In The Law of Attraction methodology, trying to figure out the how takes it out of the trust, faith, belief realm and imposes doubt (we control when we have to figure it out and that reflects doubt, worry, and fear).

Remember what it says in The Lord's Prayer in **Matthew 6:9-13**

" 'Our Father in heaven, hallowed be your name, [10] ***Your kingdom** come,*
*Your **will** be done, on earth as it is in heaven."*

Earlier I defined the Kingdom of God in **Romans 14:17** (peace and joy) and the will of God in **Ephesians 5:17** (peace, hymns, encouragement)[xviii]

So Heaven is a place of peace and joy and our prayers are for Heaven to come to earth. Jesus said in **Luke 17:21** that the Kingdom of God was within us. In essence, when we pray, we are saying that we want to vibrate high like Heaven vibrates. I believe when our vibration is high (like in Heaven) then we see the things we pray for manifest on earth.

1 Peter 3:7 says:
In the same way you married men should live considerately with [your wives], with an [c]*intelligent recognition [of the marriage relation], honoring the woman as [physically] the*

weaker, but [realizing that you] are joint heirs of the grace (God's unmerited favor) of life, in order that your prayers may not be hindered and cut off. [Otherwise you cannot pray effectively.

The word *hindered* here means to cut down a fruit bearing tree[xix]. This reminds me of the noise-cancelling headphones again. You are one with your wife and when you do not honor her (good intentions) you cut off the effectiveness of prayers (they bear no fruit) (the reverse is also true by the way) and I believe true of our children and anyone we have authority over.

Remember the faith chapters I discussed earlier. They seem to imply that we can manifest things by faith (i.e., Move Mountains). So we see this dance of the concepts of faith, asking, belief, prayer, intention, words etc. They are all interconnected. Remember the supposition that God lets the universe run to a great degree by the Law of Attraction. So prayer is an exercise of the Law of Attraction and if we follow God's criteria, we will see prayers answered. Does this build your faith in prayer?

Blessing and Scales of Justice

Old Testament law requires a thief who has been caught to repay 2 times, 5 times, or 7 times. (**Exodus 22:1; 22:4; Leviticus 6:5, 22:14, Proverbs 6:31b**) When Satan or someone steals from us, God promises to bring justice if we trust Him to bring it to pass and don't take justice into our own hands. This involves not judging (repenting) and blessing. When we judge or curse, and especially slander, we become the thief. God brings justice to our accused by blessing them and we get bad fruit. We see this illustrated in **2 Samuel 16:5-14**:

As King David approached Bahurim, a man from the same clan as Saul's family came out from there. His name was Shimei son of Gera, and he cursed as he came out.[6] *He pelted David and all the king's officials with stones, though all the troops and the special guard were on David's right and left.*[7] *As he cursed, Shimei said, "Get out, get out, you murderer, you scoundrel!*[8] *The LORD has repaid you for all the blood you shed in the household of Saul, in whose place you have reigned. The LORD has given the kingdom into the hands of your son Absalom. You have come to ruin because you are a murderer!"*

[9] *Then Abishai son of Zeruiah said to the king, "Why should this dead dog curse my lord the king? Let me go over and cut off his head."*

[10] *But the king said, "What does this have to do with you, you sons of Zeruiah? If he is cursing because the LORD said to him, 'Curse David,' who can ask, 'why do you do this?'"*

[11] *David then said to Abishai and all his officials, "My son, my own flesh and blood, is trying to kill me. How much more, then, this Benjamite! Leave him alone; let him curse, for the LORD has told him to.*[12] *It may be that the LORD will look upon my misery and restore to me his covenant blessing instead of his curse today."*

David knew this principle of justice. If they didn't retaliate, then David was set up for God to bring justice and bring a blessing.

Romans 12:19 says:

*"Do not take revenge, my dear friends, but leave room for God's wrath, for it **is** written: "It **is mine** to avenge; I will repay," says the Lord."*

When we forgive, repent for judging, bless and don't take revenge, we set ourselves up for God to bless us and take vengeance upon our enemies. But remember that they too are God's kids. (And we war not against flesh and blood) Just because it occurs to us that what they did was evil, doesn't make it so. God desires for them to come to repentance also. They will reap what they sow according to **Galatians 6:7,** so we don't have to take revenge. By staying in a state of bitterness, resentment and judgment, we ensure that we will be "turned over to the tormentors." We lower our vibration and thus should expect to reap what we sowed in our reaction to them.

Jesus said in **Luke 27-28***:*

But I say to you who are listening now to Me: [[a] in order to heed, make it a practice to] love your enemies, treat well (do good to, act nobly toward) those who detest you and pursue you with hatred, [28] Invoke blessings upon and pray for the happiness of those who curse you, implore God's blessing (favor) upon those who abuse you [who revile, reproach, disparage, and high-handedly misuse you]."

Wow – imagine how hard this is to do! But He was conferring a spiritual principle. If someone curses us, persecutes us, slanders us (remember the beatitudes in Matthew 5:11) and we do not retaliate with bitterness, hatred, judgment or cursing, then God blesses us as part of the Law of Justice. He operates within His justice system most of the time. When we go into the courtroom of Heaven, *"the accuser of the brethren"* (**Revelations 12:10**) or Satan brings our laundry list of offenses. We bring the new covenant with Jesus. This is our defense. Our sins are forgiven if we repent and forgive our offender. (According to **Mark 11:4** just quoted). This dismantles the argument of the prosecutor and God rules in our favor and awards us recompense for what was taken from us. So if we have suffered and we choose to forgive and release that "thief" and ask God for recompense, He will grant it to us. He is waiting for us to ask (words, intentions, heart desire, belief) Him to restore what was taken. Justice is a high law that seems to oversee all. Still there, but it still is not the highest law.

CHAPTER 5

THE HIERARCHIES IN THE LAWS

In the earth we see different laws in operation. The Law of Gravity keeps us from floating away. It also prevents us from flying. Yet birds and planes (and Superman) fly. The Law of Aerodynamics trumps the Law of Gravity. This suggests that laws have a hierarchy in functioning and that some laws trump others. I am sure Physicists have many examples of this. This is true in the Kingdom of God as well.

James 2:13, "Because judgment without mercy will be shown to anyone who has not been merciful. Mercy triumphs over judgment."

As we discussed, when we judge (don't show mercy) then we reap judgment (without mercy). Because of the Scales of Justice being balanced, we create a space to receive mercy and blessing when someone else judges or curses us. So mercy, which vibrates high, trumps judgment. I will call this the Law of Grace and Mercy. Grace is getting good things we don't deserve and mercy is not getting bad things we do deserve. Grace is something we live under 24/7, it never ceases. Jesus was sent to earth to pay for our sins so that we would not get what we deserved for our sins. He also gave us access to something we didn't deserve. He took the consequence eternally for our imperfections so we could be in relationship with a perfect God. In the last chapter, I explained the Law of Bitter Root Judgments as taught by Elijah House Ministries International. The Law of Sowing and Reaping would suggest that whatever bad tree was growing because of our judgments was our determined destiny in life. But **James 2:13** says the Law of Mercy trumps the Law of Judgment. When I minister to someone and we identify judgments, by forgiving the people they judged and repenting of their judgments, we make a spiritual movement towards uprooting the bad tree and making room for a new "judgment" that aligns with God's word. The Law of Mercy then triumphs. Jesus said, just after teaching "the Parable of the Unmerciful Servant," that this is how God will treat us if we don't forgive our brother or sister. Theologically, I don't believe Jesus was talking about eternal salvation. I have yet to meet a person who doesn't have some measure of unforgiveness against someone consciously or buried in their heart. I do believe he was talking about the Law of Judgments/Sowing and Reaping. As I said before, when we forgive, show mercy and bless, we get these things as well. This idea falls within the principle of "you get what you give," but the Law of Grace and Mercy trumps the Law of Judgment because eternally you don't reap the consequence of judgment, Jesus created a hierarchy to ensure that.

It says in many places in scripture, i.e., **Proverbs 3:34**; **James 4:6**; **1 Peter 5:5**: *"God opposes the proud but shows grace/favor to the humble."* (I believe this is the only place where God actually says he opposes us). (And *"pride goes before a fall,"* **Proverbs 16:18**)

In Proverbs 6:16-19, it says:

"There are six things the LORD hates,
  seven that are detestable to him:
17   **haughty eyes, (pride)**
    a lying tongue, (**speaking curse, deceit, gossip/slander**)
    hands that shed innocent blood,
18   a heart that devises wicked schemes,
    feet that are quick to rush into evil,
19   a false witness who pours out lies, (**criticism, gossip, judgment**)
    and a person who stirs up conflict in the community.
(**Gossip and judgment**).

Anytime we judge, criticize, curse, etc. we are operating in pride. Mercy and Grace trump everything. God specifically says this in a number of places in the Bible to reiterate to us that He is perfect, His love is perfect and love trumps everything. Grace is love in action. I am not sure He leaves this entirely up to a universe of laws that we can see. Humility then, seems to trump every other character quality. Humility recognizes we will forever have a log in our eye because of our imperfect human form or ego, bound in flesh. It recognizes we are forever at the favor of a Father who loves us in a way we cannot earn or deserve. It also liberates us to believe and trust him to give us what we ask for and not worry about tomorrow. If we cannot be good enough to earn his love, we can believe in unconditional love. If we get favor for no particular reason, we don't judge ourselves either. All of these laws work together to set us up for an atmosphere of high vibration.

The Law of Grace and Mercy is an inexplicable law that has no formula. This law says that sometimes you don't get consequences for your actions, and God just decides to override the laws He set forth. There are many testimonies of people getting miraculous grace directly from God. Here is an example of this:

When Tom was 14, he and his buddies were bored one night and decided to take his Dad's car for a spin. Little did they realize they would literally do that as it was very icy outside and Tom's Dad's car ended up on someone's lawn? Tom came clean and had to go to court. He had broken many laws and the normal consequence was that he would punished by not getting his D.L. until he was 18. Tom did not know the Lord but inside wished for a miracle that he would not suffer the consequence of his bad choice. In the courtroom, somehow Tom's file was lost and the case was dismissed. No one prayed for this to happen. No one begged God for mercy. No one knew to do that. God just overrode the normal process of justice and gave Tom mercy. Daily God gives us things we don't deserve and often have not known to ask for or even do correctly according to the Law of Attraction? This is grace and it comes from a real, living and a personal savior and Holy Spirit, not an impersonal universe. I know people who don't seem to practice any of these laws mentioned well and they still have favor in their lives in certain areas. Angels appearing to protect and save in some apparently random situations are the common theme of supernatural stories. It seems that sometimes God just randomly decides to give grace without explanation. But isn't that just like a Dad to do?

But perhaps there is an order to the Law of Grace and Mercy; maybe it is just too complex for our finite minds to understand or comprehend. As I stated earlier, in the field of meteorology, there is a principle called "the Butterfly Effect" which, basically concludes that, in the science of weather, the world is so intricately connected that if a butterfly in South America changes its flight pattern, it could eventually affect the weather in New York City. This is part of the Science of Chaos. Since God created the Universe and the earth, and thus the Science of Chaos, then it's not farfetched to think there might be some laws that get trumped and we simply don't know why. The Law of Grace and Mercy is one of these. Throughout scripture there are verses giving conditions for man to receive favor from God. (Not pertaining to eternal life)

But there also seems to be no particular reason why he chooses to gift and anoint certain people. We can look at all the people in the Bible and wonder, why did God choose them? No explanation. He just decides to do this. Tom had no explanation for why they lost the file – he wished for God to help him when he didn't even really know God. Shadrach, Meshach and Abednego should have burned; they did not even ask God to let them live, He just chose to send Jesus into the fire and perform a miracle. Stories about Martyrs who were burned at the stake for their faith or Christians killed in the Coliseum by Lions demonstrate that God does not always rescue. So why rescue the three Hebrews from the fiery furnace? Jonah could have died in the big fish and God sent another prophet, but God spared him. I hear stories of people in Muslim countries who have dreams where Jesus just appears to them and they give Him their life. Why them? There are stories too numerous to mention that infer God trumps His own laws sometimes, or again, perhaps He is acting in accordance with an incredibly complex formula (Science of Chaos) that no human can unravel. Perhaps one of the keys to this "formula" has to do with the prayers of other people. Quantum Physics suggests we are all interconnected. Prayer connects us instantly to someone else through intention. I don't believe we will fully understand The Science of Chaos related to God until we are in eternity and will understand all things. I believe that the principle of grace and mercy is exactly the character of God (as demonstrated by **John 3:16**) and that He wants to demonstrate to us that He sees us as sons and sometimes sons just don't get what they deserve. The love of the Father trumps the Law of Sowing and Reaping.

So perhaps the Law of Grace and Mercy exists outside of the Law of Attraction, lest we put God in a box. I believe what it really says is that the Law of Grace and Mercy stacks the odds in our favor. If the Law of Grace and Mercy were not in place, then we would always get what we deserve by our thoughts and feelings creating it. The cross ensured that the Law of Attraction had a trump card for every one of us or we would be separated from the love of God. The Bible repeatedly talks about being "*sons*" and "*co-heirs with Christ*" (**Romans 8:17**) and being "*seated in heavenly places.*" (**Ephesians 2:6**) We did not earn that position through attraction, it was a gift. By its nature, a gift is not earned.

CHAPTER 6

WHAT IS THE HEART?

"As a man thinks in his heart, so is he." **Proverb 23:7**

Earlier I quoted **Philippians 4:6-8**. I wonder how many people let something go once they pray about it. I hear lots of stories about intercession but usually intercessors feel a release and then stop praying about that thing. You may be thinking, "But what about when the issue is personal?" How many of us pray about a need or a stress but then continues to worry about how God will take care of it. I will tell a personal story. For years I was burdened for my mother to accept Christ as her savior. In 1990, I went on a fast for this. A few days into the fast, I heard an audible voice say, "It's a done deed." The burden lifted. I called my mom expecting to lead her to Christ but it did not go well. A couple years later, in an argument, I told her that the Lord told me she would give her life to Christ even though I had not yet seen it happen. Still, I never had the burden return. A couple more years went by and she did finally give her life to Christ and she told me that for years she had believed she had "grieved the Holy Spirit" at a younger age and wouldn't get another chance to receive Christ in her heart. She had spent her life staying busy in order to avoid thinking about what she thought was her certain eternal destiny. (Hell) She said that when I told her that God had told me she would find Christ, that this gave her hope. It saddened me that a misunderstood religious dogma had kept her from peace for so many years. This was a time I truly experienced **Philippians 4:6**.

One of the experiential difficulties in **Philippians 4:6** lies in truly believing God hears and/or will answer. In *The Secret*, one contributor says that to enact The Law of Attraction we are supposed to think about what we want like ordering from an online catalog. Once we really order what we want, we are supposed to let it go and then it will manifest. If we keep ordering it then we don't truly believe we will receive it. Other authors say we should continually visualize what we want and feel good as if we have received it, but we are to repeatedly practice the visualizing of what we want. There are some seeming contradictions about technique among different authors and teachers of The Law of Attraction.

The biggest challenge lies in the fact that we only are aware of about 15% of our thoughts and usually the anxiety lies in the 85% that is unconscious. (Some of that 85% is implicit memory like how to lift a glass and drink, etc.) Secondly, our trapped emotions/hurts and life experiences have caused us to mistrust that God will really answer the prayer or that we will suffer from the outcome. But truly that is what

Paul is expecting us to embrace. What about **Philippians 4:8**? Are you kidding me? Only think positive thoughts? That is impossible! But how seriously do we take this scripture? If I told people that I never think about anything bad or negative at all, almost all of the people that I know would tell me something like, "You do not live in reality then," or " that is not practical, what about all the evil, pain and suffering in the world?" But isn't this exactly what Paul is telling us to do in this scripture? Imagine if the Law of Attraction were actually really true. How much of the day do you focus on really positive **Philippians 4:8** type of things and how much do you spend thinking about negative things? Remember that there is no real distinction between prayer and thought if God is omniscient and omnipresent.

Since we are only aware of about 15% of the thoughts we have each day, the rest of our 60,000-ish thoughts are unconscious. Scientists now believe that people with ADD think maybe even millions of thoughts each day. We can make ourselves aware of some of them by paying attention to them but they are automatic. We can call this part of our consciousness, our heart.

Did you know that the heart has an electromagnetic field 60-1000 times greater than the brain? It has almost as many memory cells as the brain. It also releases hormones like the brain. It can "think" for itself. The neurons in the heart enable it to learn, remember and make decisions independent of the brain. Did you know the electromagnetic field of two people touching or within a few feet of each other, can interact so that energy activity in the heart of one person is measured in the brain waves of the other?[xx] In essence, one can "know another's heart" just by connecting.

History and language give us insight into this concept. How many words do we use every day that include the word "heart" "heartache," heartbreak," " know by heart," "in my heart," etc. We have been speaking for centuries about this idea that the heart thinks for itself. Even **Proverbs 23:7** alludes to the fact that the heart has pervasive power over our thinking. It does not say, "As a man thinks in his mind," it says, "As a man thinks in his HEART," SO IS HE. Essentially what God is telling us is that our unconscious beliefs control our life. Many psychologists have known this to be true for years.

Often the church uses the scripture **Philippians 3:13** *"Forgetting what is behind"* to tell us that inner healing or dealing with family of origin issues is not Biblical. Those in the therapy and inner healing realm know that our current perceptions and intentions for the future are dictated by our unconscious beliefs. These beliefs are formed by our life experiences, perceptions of and conclusions drawn from those experiences. Our past dictates our future by default unless we override it somehow.

It is fascinating to research heart transplant stories. These are details given by people who have received hearts from people who died. You can find these stories on the internet. Some of the results of these have shown the following:

- Heart transplant recipients gained new likes and dislikes for certain types of food.

- Heart recipient's likes for activities such as shopping, musical instruments, and types of music changed.

- One man fell in love with the widow of the man who gave him his heart. The man who died had committed suicide. The heart recipient fell in love with the widow, they married and years later, he committed suicide.

- A little girl who received a heart from another little girl who was murdered was able to identify the killer and where he lived from dreams she had after the transplant. The man confessed to killing the heart donor.

Many more of these amazing stories tell us that the heart holds keys to our very identity and thoughts. These thoughts are controlled by our past experiences, our implicit memory (the memories we develop before age 3-4 when chronological memory begins) and our trapped emotions.

Our experiences of our past shape what we believe from the time we are born and even from the womb. Quantum Physics, energy medicine and documentation from years of practice in inner healing tell us that many of our memories are formed even before birth. Science has now been able to determine that trauma and continued thought have the power to change DNA itself. Dr. Emoto's water test is now proven on another level. Trauma (negative emotions) creates a certain frequency as do words and these are now proven to impact DNA.[xxi] So our heart is not only affected by our own negative experiences but potentially by the negative experiences of our ancestors.

Muscle testing has been in practice now for several decades and has been proven valid in thousands of experiments. Muscle testing is an energy process. When our vibration changes, our physical strength changes as well. There are many commonly used and effective applications of muscle testing. Allergists find allergies by holding substances up to your body and if your muscles go weak, then that substance affects you adversely. Chiropractors find subluxations and natural practitioners find infections and organ stress. The science behind lie detector tests tells us that when we make a false statement, we vibrate lower and our muscles are weaker.

Muscle testing shows us that trapped emotions can be put into our heart from conception. The fetus in the womb absorbs emotions from its mother. Babies and young children absorb emotions experienced from their family environment. We can absorb other people's emotions that then become trapped in us at any given time. Dogs often absorb their master's emotions. Therapists and ministers know they must debrief and process this on a regular basis from the empathy they experience for clients who share intense emotions. Parents experience intense feelings from their children's experiences that can then become trapped in them.

The more intensely emotional or traumatic an experience is for us, the more likely there will be negative belief systems formed by it and corresponding trapped emotions. Trapped emotions are physical balls of low vibration energy that reside in our hearts and other parts of our bodies. We all have them and many of them. Whenever an event happens, our response will be first out of our heart. Thus our initial reaction will be based on the past experiences, unconscious beliefs and trapped emotions that are triggered by how the event "occurs" to us or how we perceive it. Nothing really occurs objectively, it is taken into the brain after being filtered by the heart and the amygdale (trauma center of the brain). How we perceive this and the meaning we give is created by these filters of past experience. We are responsible for the meaning.

Did you know that if a belief, trauma or trapped emotion occurs before the age of 4 and something occurs in the present that triggers this, it will feel as if the offense is happening right now. The hippocampus is the part of the brain that stores chronological memory. It develops between age 3-4. Before then, our memories are more like snapshots that have feelings and sensory stimulus attached to them (smell, touch, etc.). Thus it is harder to identify original trauma when it is triggered by a current event if the root belief was established at a very young age.

What this means for the Law of Attraction is that much of what we get in life is dictated by the vibration we create from these beliefs in our heart ... *"As a man thinks...."*

Teachers of the Law of Attraction make it seem easy to attract all the good things. The law says that good outweighs bad by a great deal. Some proponents believe that if 10-20% of our conscious and unconscious beliefs are positive, these will outweigh the negative and the desires of our heart will be communicated to the universe.

If we applied **Philippians 4:8** (think on good things) and **2 Corinthians 10:5** (take thoughts captive) in our conscious thoughts and **James 3:9-10** in our words, then we could make great strides in changing our vibration. This requires the discipline of focusing attention on what we are thinking and saying. It also requires us then to perform the difficult actions in the scriptures mentioned above. This is not an automatic process but has to be done with deliberation. There are many practical ways to achieve this, which will be discussed in a later chapter.

Changing the other 85% also requires deliberate effort as well. Seeking out healing for our traumas, releasing of trapped emotions and other techniques that reframe what we have believed as well as other energy release techniques, which access our unconscious, can result in noticeable changes in our thoughts, feelings and behaviors. Again, this is not easy but can result in worthwhile transformation of our heart, soul, mind and spirit.

We are body, soul and spirit and all are joined. There is not a specific delineation between these parts of man. Any changes we make in one area will affect the others as well. Nothing that occurs to us is purely spiritual, purely physical or purely soulish (mind, will and emotions). Chapter 8 will give specific ways to make these changes.

CHAPTER 7

ARE YOU A SON OR A SLAVE?

Quantum Physics says that the universe is neutral and that our lives are a creation of what we think. In the study of waves, it was discovered that when human attention was given to waves, they collapsed into particles. From this, quantum physicists (and Einstein) draw the conclusion that everything in our physical world is a creation of our (or God's) consciousness of it. Whatever a man has thought of or dreamt has eventually manifested. We can see the creation of the world as a thought of God (His consciousness) that was then created by speaking it into existence. God's creative power was then infused into man (Adam) upon creation. This is a lot to consider and accept and it may be that, like eating an elephant, you have to consume it in small bites.

But again, if we accept God's premise that, *"As a man thinks in his heart, so is he."* **Proverbs 23:7**, then the idea that we create our own reality makes sense. When we consider that thinking in our heart determines our faith and the scriptures we have discussed about asking, seeking and knocking reflect our faith, then we can conclude that in every area of our life, we choose to believe one of two options. We believe either that "the universe is for us" or that "the universe is against us." In various areas of our lives we may believe differently. For example, I am in great health, take no medications and am physically fit and more athletically inclined than most women my age. In this area it is easy to believe the universe is for me. But my past is riddled with financial struggles that seemed to contradict what I felt was my potential for success. Somewhere unconsciously I did not believe the universe was for me in the area of finances or I had an unconscious conflict with possessing wealth. This is how things occurred to me.

Scripturally we can see this same paradigm using the contrast of sons and slaves. In my experience in the church, often the teaching has focused on the idea that we are worms and worthless; that our "righteousness is as filthy rags" (**Isaiah 64:6**) and we deserve nothing good in our lives. We believe we must work really hard to show God how grateful we are for our salvation and must earn His favor by doing great works and probably suffering. Some sects of the church have used guilt and condemnation to keep us loyal to this God who demands our sacrifices and devotion. I have spent countless hours counseling and ministering to people who have embraced this paradigm of being a slave and they consistently lack joy, peace and the fruit of the Spirit. They manifest psychological, emotional and physical problems as a result of adhering to this slave mentality. Low self-esteem, self-hatred and resentments lie at the root of most relational, physical and mental illness. Is this what God intended?

I don't want to avoid the obvious theological concept throughout scripture about being a servant or slave of Christ. At first glance we might think this is a contradiction to the concept of being a son. However, I believe they are separate concepts aligning together. Perhaps the best relationship to show this alignment would be seen in the model of a king and a prince. The prince is indeed a son of the King. He is given the authority of the king and rules the kingdom as one with the king. In a loving relationship, the king loves his son as his own life and would die for him. The prince is **also** the servant of the king in that he submits to the king's decisions and rule and carries out his orders. This reflects a military position (the army of God) and relates to what we "do" without taking away from the position of son, which is who we "are." The two ideas reflect the distinction of doing vs. being. They are not mutually exclusive. Unfortunately, much of the body of Christ take on a "slave" mentality, as in unworthiness, because of "father wounds." They never truly experienced a loving father as children. They did not get the paradigm of sonship in growing up and so feel quite noble in taking on a yoke of slavery. Unfortunately, a deep seated sense of "unworthiness" is related to wounds and will not manifest fruit. I love the words of the song, "who Am I" by Casting Crowns. "Not because of who I am but because of what You've done, not because of what I've done, but because of who You are." The paradox is that we are more than worthy, but not because of anything we have or could ever do to earn it. Nonetheless, the authority of God will be manifested on the earth by **sons not by slaves** according to **Romans 8:19**.

We often over-spiritualize this idea of suffering for Jesus as being highly spiritual. But getting to serve God as a son is much more like the character of God and the model He intended when He created the family. As I see wounded people, the deepest and most life-altering changes are those that came in relationship to father and mother. God is both masculine and feminine, the embodiment of both mother and father. He created Adam and Eve in His likeness so He is both male and female. He created a model of the family to continually recreate the consciousness of the intended relationship He wants us to have with Him. Children were not created to be slaves (although in oppressed cultures they are used for this). Perhaps the best model of how God feels about us can be seen in **Luke 15:11-32**, where Jesus tells the story of The Prodigal Son. One of the most anointed teachers in my life has been Dr. George Burriss. Sitting under his teaching has been a key part of my journey into these revelations for the past two years. He is an attraction coach in Dallas, TX and a forerunner in integrating the Law of Attraction into a Biblical paradigm of life. Parts of my understanding of sonship come from one of his teachings on The Prodigal Son. (Adapted below)

Just prior to the story of The Prodigal Son, Jesus shares the Parable of the Lost Sheep and Lost Coin. In both stories, the owner of the sheep and coin leave the rest of their charge to find the one that was lost and rejoice greatly when they find it. This segues into the "Parable of the Prodigal Son." It is important that you know "prodigal" means: "characterized by profuse or wasteful expenditure or lavish or recklessly **spendthrift**"[xxii]

This is a long story but very familiar. In this story, the youngest son leaves home with his inheritance and squanders on the equivalent of booze, women and drugs. After all his money is spent and all of his "friends" leave, he cannot find a job, sleeps in the pigpen and is pretty much stripped of any remaining dignity. He returns home to beg for a slave's position in his father's house. But what happens is not what he expects.

"But, while he was still a long way off, his father saw him and was filled with compassion for him; he ran to his son, threw his arms around him and kissed him.

21 "The son said to him, 'Father, I have sinned against heaven and against you. I am no longer worthy to be called your son.'
*22 "But the father said to his servants, 'Quick! Bring the best **robe** and put it on him. Put a **ring** on his finger and **sandals** on his feet.23 bring the fattened calf and kill it. Let's have a **feast and celebrate**.24 for this son of mine was dead and is alive again; he was lost and is found.' So they began to celebrate."*

How could anyone read these three parables and not understand that Jesus is clearly telling us that God desperately loves each of his children? The robe, ring and sandals are all tokens in this culture of being a son. Each day when we cry out to God to forgive us our wrongdoings or thoughts, He, once again puts a ring, robe and sandals on us. Sons serve their father with joy and peace. Sons are provided for by their fathers. Sons are deeply and unconditionally loved. Sons walk in the love of the father. Sons vibrate high.

For many of us, we do not resonate with sonship because our parents did not model the Father's love and we have deep wounds. The other reason we do not believe we are sons can be illustrated by the older brother.

28 "The older brother became angry and refused to go in. So his father went out and pleaded with him.29 but he answered his father, 'Look! All these years I've been slaving for you and never disobeyed your orders. Yet you never gave me even a young goat so I could celebrate with my friends.30 but when this son of yours who has squandered your property with prostitutes comes home, you kill the fattened calf for him!'

Somehow the religious spirit enters the church and we forget we are sons and become slaves. We lose our love relationship with God and suddenly are driven to be good and work hard for the kingdom, forgetting to cultivate our continually transformational relationship with God. We then move back into our comfortable familiarity of the world by comparing ourselves to others. This of course leads to judgment, gossip, offense and all the things we thought we left back in the world. We become the older brother and never saw it coming.

The world we live in is a "Performance based acceptance" world. It begins as soon as we can talk and is reinforced every day, in school, work, and every arena of life. God's love is truly unconditional. He sees us as complete and whole in Christ, but we are adored simply because we are sons and are His. The minute we believe we have worked hard enough to earn the Father's approval, we become religious, we become the older son. Remember that "prodigal" means wasteful or recklessly lavish. Doesn't that sound like the story of the sinful woman and the alabaster jar in **Luke 7:36**? It was expensive and extravagant; she poured it out on him with her jar of tears also. It was wasteful. She had no one to impress, it was out of a type of gratitude only prodigals understand. God wasted Jesus' life for us. God too is a prodigal. Jesus was poured out. Remember he didn't just die for us. He was betrayed, humiliated, rejected, cursed, and tortured first. Have you ever been in love and had your heart broken? No intensity of anguish that love has ever caused us will match the feelings Jesus felt out of His love for us. Most would concur that His value was so much greater than the value of the focus of his sacrifice. (You and I) But God did not agree. Extravagance requires passion and devotion. This infers intimacy and relationship, not performance. God anguishes over wanting relationship with us.

Finally, the father wanted to throw the son a party for returning home. The older brother was mad; the father had never offered to throw him a party. The father tells him he would have gladly held a banquet if the older son had ever asked. Jesus has a perpetual banquet and feast going on (**Revelation 3:20**) with an open invitation. He perpetually wants to celebrate with us and celebrate us. Fathers don't celebrate slaves, just sons.

Ambassadors for Christ

One of the other roles of the prince is to negotiate peace. Jesus is the "Prince of Peace." Remember we said that the word "blessing" meant "God's intention" When we walk in our role as sons, we are ambassadors of peace. Our words and declarations carry the authority of the King, but He calls us specifically to walk with the intention of blessing. We are ambassadors with men and warriors with the spirits opposed to

God. We don't war with men (**Ephesians 6:12**). Sons are servants of peace with a deliberate mission to bring peace between men and God. This is a great commission as it calls us to lay our judgments, opinions and offenses aside to do the job.

The New Testament letters focus on the works and power of the Holy Spirit. Good kings delegate their authority to their sons and heirs, not to slaves. Authority is given to those who have the position to do what their leader delegates to them. Princes rode into battle to serve the kingdom of their father. They never doubted the position that they held. Princes do not question their wealth but recognize their responsibility with the management of the wealth.

This is significant when we discuss the Law of Attraction. Princes have different expectations of their life than slaves. Princes focus or give energy to different things than slaves. Princes think differently about their life than slaves. Slaves have limitations on their beliefs; Princes believe they will one day rule and reign and that all that belongs to the king is also theirs.

So, consider this: If your desire has been to walk in greater authority in the spirit realm; for your words, prayers and declarations to have a greater impact, then consider your current level of stewardship. Are the wounds of your past keeping you from staying at a place of positive "God intentions" a.k.a. blessings towards others? Could God trust you with His power and authority if your wish were to be granted? I believe that truly having a revelation of sonship is more complicated than mental agreement. It requires God rooting out the deepest places of unworthiness, shame and self-hatred. We must truly know we are loved to love others (**Matthew 22:37**). Sonship is about healing, not about knowledge. It is about relationship, not power. Sons manifest the heart of love that the father has for them and they for Him and thus for His other children.

Romans 8:14 says:

"For those who are led by the Spirit of God are the Children (Sons) of God."

Are you living a life being led by the Spirit of your Father?

CHAPTER 8

CHANGING YOUR VIBRATION

If I have effectively communicated what I believe are powerful truths in this book, then your brain should be shifting into a new paradigm (if you didn't already have it). I made this shift and it gave me the motivation I needed to work every day at making the changes in my thoughts, words and actions to stay at a high vibration. When we start something new, we have to work at it consciously until we become consciously competent at it and then eventually we do it automatically and have unconscious competence. I desperately want God to trust me with His authority. I desperately want people to be healed in my presence. It is my call and my passion. I desperately want to see the Kingdom of God manifested on earth. If you can see these truths then the following are practical steps on changing your life. They are deliberate and some require more energy than others. But the fruit will be worth the effort.

Anything that makes you feel down lowers your frequency. Here is a list of what I have found lowers frequency: [xxiii]

- **Control and Resistance**–Control or manipulation of others or situations is motivated out of fear and worry. Fear of being controlled by others, even God, also lowers frequency. Fear is low vibration and will never produce good fruit.

- **Judgments, curses, resentment**– As we discussed in that chapter, these are low vibration thoughts and words that attract negative things. Feelings of fear, anxiety, depression, anger, guilt, shame, jealousy, and envy all have a low frequency. When they are trapped they contribute to belief systems which are negative. (The universe is against me) Whether we are committing these in thought or deed against ourselves or others, all are lowering frequency.

- **Alcohol, Prescription and Recreational drugs**– Although these may make you feel better temporarily, they lower frequency and are not legitimate ways to reduce stress.

- **Food** - Fresh, live food has a high frequency, but processed foods have a low frequency and lower the frequency of your body. Pesticides and toxins lower frequency.

- **Lack of exercise, sleep, and water**–Not taking care of our physical needs lowers frequency

- **Negative environment**–Other people's frequencies can raise or lower our own depending on the situation. Gossip, judging, pessimism, and fear-mongering lower our vibration and frequency

Changing Conscious Beliefs, Words, Thoughts, and Vibration

I want to challenge you for a minute. How teachable are you? Most of us think we are teachable but change happens when we decide we are willing to do whatever it takes to truly change and we take deliberate steps to do that. Change is not rapid, we are not wired for rapid change, and our brain cannot manage it. But deliberate and steady steps to change make a huge impact on our vibration and will get us to our goals. Take a few minutes and consider your willingness to change before you take this on.

I have discussed **2 Corinthians 5:10, Philippians 4:6-8, James 3:9-10** and other scriptures we all know and read. The real issue is that we are not self-conscious of what we think because we allow our unconscious to rule our lives. Becoming aware of what we think takes practice. Challenging our thoughts once we are aware of them takes practice. When you read the chapter on Bitter Root Judgments, did you realize that you probably were not even aware that you judged people constantly? So the key to changing conscious beliefs is really about being self-aware. The other motivation is about accepting as truth the paradigm laid out in this book. If you don't truly believe that everything you think, believe and say dictates the course of your life, then you won't make the effort to change it. We all put energy into things that matter to us and motivate us. If you are truly motivated to change your life, then you will put energy into changing your vibration. Here are some ways you can do this:

1. **Take worry captive.** Worry is a form of fear and control and vibrates low. I want to share a key story in my life. I grew up with the unconscious message "responsible people worry." My whole life I believed this was true. I knew about **Matthew 6** and that worrying was not trusting God but I didn't know how to stop worrying. After getting the **Romans 14:17** revelation in George Burriss's Bible Study, I understood that worry was producing the opposite results that I wanted to achieve by worrying. This was especially true in the area of finances. I also wanted very much to reflect the Kingdom of God. Once I

understood that the most effective place I could be for God and attract the best things in my life was peace, joy, love, and gratitude, I had the motivation I needed to take worry captive with vigor!

2. **Practice gratitude**. All of the fruit of the Spirit measure on a high-frequency wavelength. Gratitude also helps us shift our thoughts when we are stuck in the negative. When we think negatively, we send out a low attraction to attract more negative. The Law of Attraction doesn't know the word, "don't." Whatever you think about is what you attract. So think about what you want, not what you don't want. Disciplining yourself to practice the art of gratitude every day is very beneficial. The Bible tells us to "put on a garment of praise for a spirit of heaviness" (**Isaiah 61:3**)

3. **Smile for a minute or two**. You cannot think negatively when you are truly smiling. Include things in your life that make you laugh and smile frequently.

4. **Avoid negative news and allow other people to have a different perception or opinion than you...** I don't watch the news at all, nor do I engage in political discussions or arguments. Everyone is entitled to an opinion and a perception. In many arenas, there is not a right or wrong, there are perceptions and opinions. Different perceptions keep us open to evaluating what

we truly believe and adhere to and trust (remember the definition of belief or faith). While the tenets of Christianity are generally agreed upon through most denominations, many other areas are cause for dissension, disagreement and judgment. I once read a quote by Rick Joyner regarding this. He said, "In the main tenets (of Christianity, there should be unity, in the fringe areas liberty and in ALL things, charity (love). We should love everyone whether or not they agree with our doctrine. Take each one of the parts of **Philippians 4:8** and practice it. Think of something good; then think of something lovely; and so on. These are the practices which change your thinking. Insert your name into the scripture – "I am good, lovely ..."

5. **Avoid negative people, Choose people (or pets) who celebrate you**. This is not entirely possible all the time but within the realm of what you do have power to do, surround yourself with affirming, encouraging people who see the glass half – full (or overflowing). I have certain opinions about things but I rarely engage in arguments. I don't believe there has to be a wrong and right. Debate is a power struggle to make someone wrong. This tends to create a low vibration atmosphere. It's ok on occasion, but pay attention to the fruit of the spirit and see if you really feel this

manifesting fruit. We are more powerful when we enable other people to also be powerful. Remember the definition of God's will: **Ephesians 5:17-20**

[17] Therefore do not be vague and thoughtless and foolish, but understanding and firmly grasping what the will of the Lord is. [18] And do not get drunk with wine, for that is debauchery; but ever be filled and stimulated with the [Holy] Spirit. [19] Speak out to one another in psalms and hymns and spiritual songs, offering praise with voices [[c]and instruments] and making melody with all your heart to the Lord, [20] At all times and for everything giving thanks in the name of our Lord Jesus Christ to God the Father." Most theologians will tell you they rarely won someone to the Lord with a theological argument. Love is more powerful than being right. Pets always love us and celebrate us. Studies show that having pets is an effective way to lift depression in people.

6. **Forgive quickly when someone hurts you and choose to bless them; repent of judging them.** Pay attention to the thought, "I would never do that." Pay attention to the thoughts that you feel superior or inferior to someone in any area – these are low vibration thoughts. When you catch yourself doing this, take those thoughts captive. One of the things I love most about

my friends is they say amazing things to encourage me (words of affirmation is one of my love languages) and often it disarms me because I realize that my unconscious belief does not align with how they see me. I want to believe about myself what they say about me. I can't tell you how immediately I feel my vibration change because I know these people really know me and love me and really believe what they are saying. Being around people who love you is a great way to change your beliefs about yourself and raise your vibration.

7. **Memorize or have access to scripture**. When we catch our self-thinking something that contradicts what God says about us, it is a great resource to immediately know the scripture we want to use to challenge that belief. Taking time to know scripture is helpful to take thoughts captive. Buy a book of God's promises or keep daily devotionals readily available. I have a list of God's promises He has made to me personally that I remind Him and myself of each day. We don't actually have to remind God, He has not forgotten, but, like Jacob, there is the issue of contending for Him to bless us. Reminding Him that He has promised to bless us is creating and declaring and contending for our promise.

8. **Begin to develop the disciplines of meditation or contemplative prayer**. These help us to become more aware of what we are thinking. Take whatever steps necessary to learn to quiet your mind. Learn from another person who seems to have mastered this art and ask them to help you. Go to meditation or contemplative prayer groups and soaking prayer groups. Practice tuning yourself into the Holy Spirit each day and choosing to think very deliberate thoughts. Learn how to sit quiet self and listen to Him. I admit I am one of the ADD people who have a million thoughts every day. My best time to listen is when I first wake up and when I am driving. God speaks to me on road trips like no other time and He seems to speak to me often around 3 am by awaking me suddenly. At these times my mind is less active and I am more peaceful. Take time to choose what to think.

9. **Learn visualization techniques.** This involves a deliberate use of our seeing and feeling imagination. Imagine what you want your life to look like. Speak what you visualize, (hearing) feel it and see yourself doing it. This builds faith for a positive future to change your beliefs about your future. Studies show that the brain cannot distinguish between visualizing in detail with emotion attached and actually experiencing

something. It registers the same on scales of measurement. When our brain experiences something as "real" then our faith for that thing is built. Ministers will often visualize how they want the service to go and it encourages belief for miracles and for God to move mightily. Take time to choose what you think. Earl Nightingale[xxiv] made a recording in 1956 after reading Napoleon Hill's book, *Think and Grow Rich*[xxv] and having the revelation "We become what we think." He combined Hill's book with the two scriptures "As a man thinks... and you reap what you sow"...He became wealthy from this recording and all the "Secret Societies" know this "secret" principle. The body of Christ has had access to the most profound secrets to living for thousands of years and the secular world seems to better apply these to their lives than we do as Christians. CHOOSE WHAT YOU THINK AND THINK WHAT YOU CHOOSE.

10. **Take time to make very deliberate affirmations of self** (As a man thinks...). I have found a meditation called "The Moses Code" that uses "I am" statements. "I am that I am" is the name of God. (**Exodus 3:14**) While we are not saying we are God, we are made in His image and likeness (**Genesis 1:27**) We use "I am" statements because there is the Power of the Holy Spirit

dwelling in us and that power is the power to create and change. When Jesus said, "I am" in the Garden of Gethsemane. (**John 18:5**) The power of his words caused the army to fall back. Agreeing with what God says about us in our "I am" statements, (i.e. I am abundant, I am highly favored, I am peace, I am joy, I am loved, I am successful, etc.) align with the scriptures we have discussed in this book. I speak the desires of my heart and the promises of God. Any area my faith seems to be faltering is a focus of my "I Am" statements. I can feel myself returning to a state of faith and trust (and joy) from states of distress when I do this.

11. **Spend time with the Lord/Holy Spirit in worship.** We want to spend time soaking in God's presence and feeling His tangible love for us. However you experience feeling connected to God then make time to do it. (Music, journaling, reading, praying, listening to teaching, etc.) This is a non-doing, non-performing time. This is a receiving affirmation time.

12. **Avoid situations that create *"ought to, should, need to"* obligations.** Changing beliefs means relieving oneself of the "have to" performance mentality in life. Remember our intention is EVERYTHING. The

motive of everything we do is what creates the attraction.

13. **Choose your commitments**. If you make a commitment then you choose to fulfill it – it is not an obligation but a commitment that you chose.

14. **Take care of your brain**. As I already stated, we are body, soul and spirit. Perhaps the most overlooked, ignored and minimized part of our thinking is the physiological. Our brain is a complex organ that requires good nutrition to function. Most of us can find addiction in our ancestry which speaks of a generational inheritance of low serotonin and imbalances in other brain neurochemicals. The stress of life, diet/malnutrition, lack of exercise and toxic environment add to this problem. Trapped emotions directly affect our serotonin and dopamine balances. Believers especially tend to ignore this. No one talks about the epidemic of depression, anxiety, ADHD and other life-altering disorders. Your brain chemistry directly affects your vibration. Depressed people are hard pressed to think happy thoughts and be grateful. Anxious people can't return to peace and joy. OCD sufferers cannot master their thought life. The church as a whole and the general population must embrace this third part of our being. Learning to be attuned to

your brain chemistry and educating yourself about what nutritional supplements could be taken is critical to being successful. Even the masters of the Law of Attraction rarely talk about this. Ask any woman who is PMS-ing or in menopause if they think and possibly behave differently at this time and they all agree they become a different person. Ask someone with ADD or Bi-polar how easy it is to control anger and impulses. Only someone who has suffered can relate to the challenge of any of these suggestions when their brain chemistry is not balanced. Our brain needs adequate nutrition. Our brain desires homeostasis. It will use whatever memories or thoughts that have worked in the past to feel "normal" Addicts will crave whatever drug makes them feel "normal" Even the most seemingly sane and happy people who smoke will tell you how nearly impossible it is to calm anxiety without a cigarette. Consult a natural doctor, take the right supplements, exercise, eliminate white sugar, rest, relax, have fun and generally take care of yourself. Princes know that to become King, they must take care of themselves first. We desire for people to want what we have (Christ). If we are not truly walking in joy and peace, then all of the "good works" we do will not have the impact of someone who takes care of themselves first. Vessels of light and power vibrate high. You cannot short circuit making this happen and you cannot fake a vibration. We are creatures made out of energy remember, so intuitively we sense the vibration of another and know truth. The gospel is caught by shining our light. Make managing your own brain chemistry a priority.

15. **Decide to always pause and check our hearts before we speak**. This itself is quite a discipline. Remember if we really believe our words have power and authority (as sons) then choosing to not respond out of emotions but to pause and wait is a powerful tool to maintain integrity and a high vibration. We have all been damaged by people's words and surely don't really want to damage someone else out of our hurt and anger. Remember intention and motive determine fruit. Do we want everything burned as wood, hay and stubble because we were hasty to respond out of our emotions? I am continually learning that I must return to joy before I engage in a conversation with someone even if it means that there is a delay in resolving a situation. I have only learned that from failure time and time again to do so. But because of my profession and my desire to stay at joy and peace, I have made some commitments in my life to be this way.

16. Examine the meaning you have given to a situation.
If you accept the paradigm that in most of life, there is
not objective truth, only our perceptions and the
meaning we give them, then we can choose to examine
our perceptions before we react to an event. We decide
that what we feel and believe is our responsibility and
possibly ask ourselves the question, "Where does this
feeling come from and is my response out of fear or
love?" In any situation there is "what happened" (i.e.,
John stepped on my toe) and the meaning I gave it.
(John is mad at me). This is what I mean by
perception. The meaning I give it determines whether
or not I take offense. Is my response empowering or
damaging to the other person? In our moments of joy
and peace, we do not want to hurt anyone else and we
want to empower them. We lose that motive when our
hurts have been triggered. We all get triggered and
even when we are seeking healing for our triggers; this
is only progressive and never absolute. Taking a time
out while in a state of heightened emotion will prevent
us from damaging ourselves and others. Seeking only
ways to return to joy and/or peace from distress needs
to be our priority. Wait to speak until you know your
intention is leaning towards love, hope or peace. This
is a very different paradigm from the way most people

think and live. But our unconscious was programmed during a state of heightened emotion so keeping our heart safe means we retreat when this state reoccurs. As sons of God, our goal is to be "unoffendable." While we will always be confined to a body and battle fleshly desires, working towards releasing trauma, trapped emotions and judgments from our past (discussed in next section) move us towards a position of love.

17. **Determine to stay humble and teachable.** If we listen to others with the intent to learn rather than teach, argue or be right, then we are always learning and are less likely to move into a state of control. Remember that *"God resists the proud but gives grace to the humble." (James 4:6)*

18. **Educate yourself about using essential oils.** In the expanding world of understanding vibration, the use of essential oils in healing continues to gain momentum. As I shared earlier, there are great benefits to essential oils and they can definitely aid in raising your vibration.

19. **Eat good food, drink enough water**. Every living thing has a vibration. If we put high vibration food into our bodies, we raise our frequency. Our bodies cry out for water every day (not soda, juice etc which are

processed and have a lower frequency). Foods with chemicals, white sugar, and highly processed foods have a low vibration so eat food as close to its original state as possible.

20. **Get adequate sleep, exercise, fun and rest.** We must take care of our temples to function well. Remember our goal is the Kingdom of God. Exercise outside to get sun (Vitamin D) and fresh air. It is said that salt air has healing properties. Fun decreases stress and depression. Creative ventures (music, art, dance, etc.) use a part of the brain which promotes well-being.

21. **Take supplements, EMF protectors, cleanses, get Chiropractic care, have massage therapy and more.** We must put in good, necessary high-vibration elements and eliminate toxic, low vibration things. Supplements help keep the body in healthy vibration. Electromagnetic frequency absorbers block the damaging waves we get from computers, microwaves, cell phones and all electronics. Cleanses and colonics help the body dump low vibration toxins. . Subluxations and trapped energy flow bring down the vibration so wellness and caring for every system of our body keeps us at maximum physical potential.

As we take on a discipline of changing our conscious beliefs, it will segue into also changing our unconscious ones as well. If we think of our brain as a map of neuronal pathways that fire rapidly, then our thinking becomes akin to taking a certain route to work every day. We can almost make this trip with our eyes closed because it is so habitual. This same thing occurs in the pathways in our brain and they are actually burned strongly like "ruts."

If we were traveling to work one day and the road was closed due to construction, we would then have to take a detour which would require us to pay attention and think. It takes very deliberate effort to change these ruts in our brain but when we successfully do it, we find a new path gets burned. The more we practice our new routes, and then they become ruts but positive ones. (Like if we deliberately practiced **Philippians 4:8.**)

Steps to Change Our Unconscious Beliefs

If you study cults and developed methods of brainwashing you will find there are well-developed procedures for programming the mind. Satanic ritual abuse involves repeated trauma starting at a young age. A child's brain dissociates under certain amounts of real or perceived threats. In this state of dissociating, new information can be programmed into the mind. Cults cause dissociation in children, forming multiple parts and then give these parts secret information useful only to the cult but threatening for anyone else to know. That part is then triggered to manifest under certain conditions when that information is important. The military use of brainwashing and the controversial MKUltra conspiracy are also fascinating to study. Novels and movies Like *The Bourne Trilogy* and *Manchurian Candidate* prompt us to consider the accessibility of the unconscious. Once belief systems are created and reinforced, they may become very stable, even if irrational. If emotions are intense enough, the abuse victim's brain will completely disconnect from the occurrence of the event using repression or amnesia of the event, but leaving behind the belief system. In the brain, the hippocampus is responsible for chronological or explicit memory. The amygdale is the part of the brain that is looking out for danger. If the amygdale decides something is dangerous enough, it is not allowed into the hippocampus. Many traumatic events are not easily accessed by conscious memory but definitely stored in the unconscious. Again using the concept of heart memory also, everything is recorded somewhere within our being. (This is another discovery in Quantum Physics) When this belief or memory is triggered, the body reacts as if it is happening in that moment. Soldiers manifesting PTSD are certain someone is watching them at all times and they are in certain danger. Their hyper-vigilance is a manifestation of a deep unconscious belief system programmed when they were truly unsafe and in a heightened state of emotion. All of us have this occurring to some degree although possibly not in such an extreme fashion. Someone may be terrified of dogs with no recollection of why, but it is highly likely somewhere they felt very threatened by a dog at sometime in their life when they felt were without defense. Their amygdale may have prevented the information from being stored in the hippocampus but it is stored as energy in the subconscious or heart and occurs as an unconscious belief that dogs are mean and threatening.

We can use this same information to very deliberately move towards reprogramming our unconscious from negative to positive. I have outlined three steps towards this:

1. **Release trapped emotions, vows and judgments.** After years of working in inner healing and psychology, I have come to understand the following process: Our painful experiences create judgments, vows and deep rooted belief systems about our self, others, God and "the universe." As I just stated, this occurs when there is heightened emotion. The situation does not have to necessarily be traumatic but just heightened. Most of these occur during times of heightened negative emotions. Prayer ministry and muscle testing help uncover those deeply rooted judgments and beliefs that control our unconscious belief systems. Our emotions follow our beliefs and that affects behavior and it affects vibration and thus, attraction. As I

explained in the Bitter Root Judgments chapter, we attract from our judgments. The problem is finding those judgments. When they are deeply rooted, we don't even know we believe them. After years of being involved in this ministry, I still felt there were pieces missing as I watched people's lives after receiving ministry. I saw that people got immediate relief but after some time passed, they went back to many of the same old belief systems. One of these pieces of the puzzle manifested to me when I learned about trapped emotions. Negative emotions get physically trapped within those belief systems during the state of heightened emotions and they occur as low vibration balls of energy, physically trapped. I had spent many hours over the course of years releasing judgments (I really had a lot against my mother and my brother) but I still noticed that I had pain attached to many memories. I also noticed that all the good decisions I had made to replace the judgments had not completely bloomed, although I did see some good fruit in my life. When I started releasing the trapped emotions, I found a new level of peace. This trapped emotion release was necessary for me to take captive thoughts of worry. We don't control our fear reactions (or they wouldn't be reactions) I believe that trapped emotion work is critical to experience true peace and joy. As a highly empathetic person, I felt and feel everything intensely; both my emotions and those of other people and had spent the first 21 years of my life stuffing them. This step made an opening for me to reprogram my heart/unconscious with new beliefs. I had tried some reprogramming techniques already but I discovered it seemed they weren't taking root like I had hoped until I started releasing the trapped emotions. One of my habits now is when I am laying out my requests before the Lord and then using attraction/prayer techniques, I test myself if there are any trapped emotions that would keep me from truly believing this thing would come to pass. The answer seems to always be "yes" and I always find there are judgments that prevent me from believing I can have the things I desire and want. Often the memories are not highly traumatic but have caused me to form a judgment about life (or the universe), myself, God, etc. Almost every day, God reveals some new area in my life that is driven by subtle beliefs that don't align with His truth. It is a lifelong journey of transformation. An example of this that I encounter often is related to women who can't seem to lose weight or keep it off. Dieting doesn't seem to work. When I look for the trapped emotions creating this circumstance, I typically find patterns of experiences related to rejection, abandonment, abuse and failure. The weight is a consequence of a series of unconscious beliefs and judgments. It is not going to be fixed with food. Every issue in our lives has trapped emotions and negative belief systems as part of the root system. Another common area is about believing one is attractive to the opposite sex. No matter how many scriptures we quote, self-deprecating thoughts and feelings seem to dominate. I usually find many experiences of rejection or humiliation creating a mosaic of unconscious beliefs that not only keep someone from feeling beautiful but, because of the laws in place, prevent that person from attracting the kind of person they truly want to be with.

2. **Make space for new unconscious belief systems.** Even though I had recognized the judgments and vows, there had still been a block to access and create the possibility of change. Once the trapped emotions and the vows, curses and judgments are released, we have to fill that space with a new belief system. This is reprogramming. If we don't do this, then the void will just be filled with what was familiar and comfortable. Something will happen to cause us to recommit the same judgments and vow the same things we just broke in order to refill that void. In terms of the Law of Attraction, right after releasing the old, we can start visualizing and attracting the new, but the time delay

between the old vibration and the new may still allow for negative things to come to us. The familiar negative belief and the trapped emotion will draw back the old system. I have seen that on average it takes a few months after doing trapped emotions sessions for there to be a truly distinct pattern of fruit to be seen. Reprogramming is deliberate. This was another missing piece that I had seen from some of the inner healing models that I had implemented and had seen others go through. New beliefs were stated, but the practice of rooting them deeply was not accomplished. Often Christians are told by Christian Counselors to just read more scripture, pray more etc. to solve our deeply rooted problems. Most of the people who end up in a therapist's office claim that this process didn't work. The truth is not that scripture or praying wasn't helpful, but that the distress in their hearts/unconscious prevented them from changing their deep-rooted thoughts. The trapped emotions and beliefs were not accessible by the left brain (used in memorizing). While declarations are powerful (authority), if the unconscious is resolute in its belief systems, the left brain loses the battle. So the follow up is the key.

3. **Find techniques that deliberately reprogram the unconscious.**

The next step after making space is to create new Godly beliefs (ones that line up with God's word). Once established, the crucial element is to follow up on a regular basis with some of the deliberate or conscious techniques mentioned, "I am" statements, meditation, etc. "Attraction Coaches" specialize in changing unconscious belief systems. The world of motivational speakers is full of advice on how to change your world. But gathering more information is limited in its effect on the unconscious. The effective workshops include bringing the participant to a heightened state of emotion. Part of the process that I do in Prayer ministry involves establishing new belief systems based on what we have just "planted" in the space left by removing judgments. Still, using daily techniques to water the seeds planted must be implemented. This is not exclusive of others, just ones that have worked for me and from reports of other people. I cannot endorse the effectiveness beyond techniques I myself have tried. There are certainly many others of which I am not aware. Visualizing changes both the conscious and unconscious belief systems. While we create new ideas and imaginations in our conscious mind, visualizing and creating vivid images **also produce a positive heightened emotion (instead of negative).** This allows an inroad into that space left from removal of the old and waters that new belief seed. If you didn't feel loved by mom and we release some of that pain, bitterness and judgment regarding this and then you spend time visualizing yourself as a child and feeling loved by your mom, in effect you can rewrite history to create a new program deep within your heart of a world where mom loved you. That may seem odd, but remember that when you visualize your brain can't distinguish between reality and imagination. Inviting the Holy Spirit into the memory is also a frequently used approach to healing that memory as God's presence may produce a vision of Him being present with His love. This has the same effect but is even more powerful as it comes from an omnipresent source of love.

I want to share a very personal story of how quickly I was reprogrammed by a new thought. Over the years, I have spent many hours going through healing of my hurts and uprooting judgments. Objectively speaking, my childhood was not that traumatic but I am a highly sensitive person so everything that occurred in my life created trapped emotions. Many of the hours I spent healing related to the hurt I felt from my mother. I had truly forgiven her, made space for many new good trees and repented of judgments towards her. My mom had died of cancer but between diagnosis and death, we had some wonderful times of restoration. Still, in my unconscious, I didn't realize that I didn't believe she really had loved me as a child. One day I was reviewing the "five love languages."[xxvi] My love languages are "physical touch" and "words of affirmation." (The other three languages are "gifts," "quality time" and "acts of service.") I was meditating on my children's love languages and the realization that I was not deliberate about speaking to them in their languages. I had a sudden revelation that my mom's love languages were quality time and gifts. Suddenly deep in my spirit, my heart went from not feeling loved by her to knowing I was loved. In a flash I relived all the time she spent playing board games with me or teaching me card games, reviewing classic books, ballroom dancing, taking me shopping etc. My whole childhood was relived in a moment. I had made space and planted trees, but in this moment I relived my childhood from a consciousness of being loved.

Another way to reprogram the unconscious is demonstrated in the book The Healing Code[xxvii] by Alex Loyd. I began to practice healing codes. I found them very effective at relieving distress and felt the energy flowing through my body. They involve energy points in the head area related to speaking positive affirmations and visualizing positive images. The theory is that by doing this while connected to the body's energy system, the intentions and images go deeper into the subconscious. Dr. Loyd is a strong Christian who gives much of his proceeds to ministry. His book is worth reading. I have a number of very specific promises God has shown me and I use these as part of my Healing Code process so I know I am stating both the desires of my heart and what I believe is my destiny and God's will for my life.

Words are the language of the soul, images are the language of the spirit and sounds are the language of the body. When we use techniques that involve all three of these elements, we engage body, soul and spirit to the things we desire. I have also used a process called the "Immune System Master Key" also by Alex Loyd also which uses words relating to God, sounds/music and images to have a trifecta effect on the whole person.

Declare God's promises continually as part of what you visualize. Remember the repeated premise of this book includes the power of thought, emotion and words to bring transformation. Declarations are powerful. The same power that created the universe (the Holy Spirit) dwells in you. Whether or not you are part of an arena of the body of Christ that believes in, practices or operates in the prophetic, I have never met a Christian who does not believe that God has promised them something specific. How God communicated that to them may vary from person to person but everyone believes God has put something strongly in their spirit. Most people can quote **Psalms 37:4**, "Delight yourself also in the lord and he will give you the desires and secret petitions of your heart." They have secret desires they are hoping for God to fulfill as they seek Him. Remember that feeling what you want and visualizing is key to changing your unconscious beliefs, vibration and attraction.

Our heart speaks to God its desires but often they contradict its beliefs. Sons believe loving fathers will give them their desires. When we review our beliefs and challenge them (often this requires another person or counselor) we often see that our core beliefs about what we deserve do not line up with our desires. Our "faith" or theology may be overriding our desires.

When I am using my various techniques for getting to my unconscious, I often quote some of the Bible's promises from God, special scriptures and revelations I have received and some the personal promises of God to me. I do this because I want to continually be reprogramming my core belief system to a paradigm in which I believe God loves me and knows what's better for me than I know. My desire is for my will to align with His will and to be obedient. The Biblical principle of the prophetic word is that speaking it brings it from Heaven to Earth and its declaration makes it available to come to pass. By declaring the words and promises that I believe that God has declared for my life, then I believe it is more likely that they align with "the desires of my heart" and not conflict. My spirit has received these words as promises and then can broadcast them with faith. I use my personal words and coinciding emotions while doing healing codes.

CHAPTER 9

YOU CAN CHANGE THE WORLD

Have you ever been in a large crowd and it made you realize how small and insignificant you really were? I have often wondered what difference I can truly make in the world. Yes I realize I am important to my children and my friends. I realize that in my ministry experience and profession, if I look back, God has used me to impact people's lives in a positive way and all of that felt really good. However, that good feeling faded quickly as I realized the past successes never satisfy for long in this linear time line.

A few years ago, there was a TV series called, "Heroes." One of the main characters was named "Claire" and played by the actress Hayden Panettiere. She was a teenager who couldn't die and she would self heal. (Unless her head was either cut off or her brain was punctured) In the fall of 2007, the catch-phrase advertising for the show was, "Save the cheerleader, save the world." This phrase made reference to the story line that somehow Claire would "save the world" and another character, Hiro (who could time travel), had received a personal message given to him and his mission was to find and save the "cheerleader."

As I was preparing this book, I thought about that catch phrase. What is a cheerleader? A cheerleader is someone who doesn't look at the reality of a situation (i.e., the football game) and whose job it is to speak possibility with great enthusiasm. She/he is, in fact, a Pollyanna whose job is to stay positive and never give up hope. Cheerleaders speak blessings and victory. They do not judge the character or performance of their team; they only encourage and speak possibilities.

I believe that this phrase was a prophetic call to the body of Christ. Each one of us has an inner cheerleader somewhere inside. If you have concluded the concept of the Law of Attraction is true, then what might be some implications if we truly practiced it? What if we deliberated to take our thoughts captive (**2 Corinthians 10:5**) and practice **Philippians 4:8** to only think on good things? Imagine if we stopped several times a day and truly repented for judging someone? (Including politicians, preachers, our parents or our kids) What if then we turned around and blessed them? Can you imagine embracing a paradigm of seeking hard after getting our root issues, emotions and irrational belief systems exposed and transformed? What if your attitude towards life every day was about everything that happened being purposeful in God's transformation process in your life? Imagine spending your time visualizing a world full of God's love, peace and power (like a cheerleader) instead of focusing on all the evils in the world. What if the Law of Attraction were true? If we successfully did this even 51% of the time, I believe the following would result:

- We would stay in a state of joy and peace which IS the Kingdom of God. All our needs would be met. We would enjoy each day to the fullest because we were not worrying about tomorrow.

- We would be in Gods will according to **Ephesians 5:17-20**.

- By quickly taking negative thoughts about others captive and choosing to bless them, we would reap blessing and not the Law of Bitter Root Judgments. There would be less "bad fruit" in our lives.

- By thinking only positive about ourselves, we would move towards believing we are sons and not slaves. Remember, sons walk in God's authority and manifest signs and wonders and the glory of God. Imagine how we would change the world if we truly walked in God's power all the time. What if the "greater works" Jesus was talking about (**John 14:12**) were available to us and the only reason we aren't walking in signs and wonders is because of the blocks we have in our beliefs and we are reaping from our judgments?

- By practicing the technique of visualization and focusing our attention and intention or prayer on the solution and not the problem, we could manifest a world that is full of God's Holy Spirit, righteousness, peace. What we give energy to expands and grows. (By focusing on, talking about and thinking about the evil in the world, we bring our vibration down, give energy to and empower evil to grow)

- Because we are all interconnected, our higher vibration raises the vibration of the whole world. One individual matters.

Do you know that, according to teachings I have heard from Kevin Trudeau's tapes "Your Wish is my Command," that all of the "secret societies" (i.e., skull and crossbones, Masons, Illuminati, The Brotherhood) have known this information for decades and practice it as a means of securing and maintaining wealth. These groups are not professing Christians and may serve other gods. Do you understand what this means? The followers of other gods, not the one True Lord Jesus, have mastered the art of "prayer" (thought, intention, visualizing) and practice it as part of their lifestyle. They expect this application of the Law of Attraction to work for them on a regular basis and it does. Most of them have **greater faith** in "the universe" via the Law of Attraction than the Church has in a loving God. The one thing they lack is the supernatural power of the cross to exert forgiveness and love from the spirit and (more importantly) a real relationship with a living God. WAKE UP believers! We have access to the Most High God through prayer, thought and intention and we have the power and authority to change the world as sons of the one and only King. We are not using this power effectively as a whole. By taking on these truths, we get to be participants in the greatest move of God in history.

Imagine if believers all over the world took the scriptures I have discussed in this book seriously and made **Philippians 4:6-8, Ephesians 5:17-20, Matthew 7:1**, and **2 Corinthians 10:5** a priority each day. What do you think we, as a unified corporate body, could manifest in the world? The unity of believers is the constant target of Satan's attack because He knows the truths mentioned in this book and The Book. Individually, if we determined to walk in love for God, ourselves and others (by practicing these scriptures, deliberating to get free from our trapped emotions, traumas, judgments and vows, forgiving and blessing quickly and walking as Sons of a living God) we would truly change the world. God tells us throughout scripture that we have the power and authority to change the world.

Often people don't understand why they should go back through their life and review their history. Critics often call this "navel gazing" because it requires intense focus inward. But sons of the King know they will rule one day and they live their life with this in mind, they aspire to become the best rulers they can become. They are more concerned with who they are than what they do. We are to embrace a life paradigm that involves allowing our wounds to be triggered in order to reveal where our unconscious (and conscious) beliefs do not align with God's word. This creates a life of constant transformation and the ability to see all occurrences as potential for transformation and blessing. Ironically, many of the naysayers have had truly painful childhoods and just don't want to believe they have to revisit any of that. But we are creatures of God's light and the Holy Spirit and all the trapped emotions inside lower the intensity of our light in daily interaction. Under the power of the anointing we may shine brightly, but in the context of our day-to-day relationships, we stay in fleshly coping mechanisms because our wounds are being triggered daily by life's events.

Maybe Mark Twain had more of a clue about God than he has been accredited. He wrote:

Sing like no one's listening, love like you've never been hurt, dance like nobody's watching, and live like its heaven on earth. Get busy vibrating high!

Summary
(A Call to Action)

I have spent twenty years in an ebb and flow of healing and transformational processes. It has frustrated me to no end to see this process happen much more slowly than I had desired. In the past two years, where I have discovered the missing puzzle pieces discussed in this book, I have truly felt an acceleration of the deep-level changes I had hoped for. Perhaps the very deepest key was realizing that, in many areas, I did not believe God or the universe was truly for me and therefore continued to expect suffering, pain and constant trials. After all, Paul suffered tremendously, as do saints all over the world. I am not saying that God is not intently bringing us to transformation but the topic of suffering is truly debated Biblically. There are many metaphors that suggest we must go through some painful things in life to become equipped as sons of God. The Bible uses the image of gold going through fire to be purified, the image of a vine being pruned, the image of being crucified (our flesh) and others. I also like the metaphor of the olive. The olive (us) must be pressed for the oil (the anointing) to be extracted. The flesh or ego screams for power daily. Understanding that everything that happens ultimately brings us to transformation is helpful in rejoicing in all things. However, I must admit, for many years I was at odds with God. How could someone who said He loved me so much allow constant pain to occur? As many hours as I spent in His presence, I drew the conclusion of Job; *"Though You slay me, yet I will hope in You."* (**Job 13:15**) I experientially understood God to be a God of healing my hurts and wounds and had experienced the restoration of lost things with the memories of pain being erased. But on a deep level, I wasn't sure I really trusted Him. I realize I had an expectation of suffering and pain so I got what I expected to get. The spiritual pride in me created a belief that spiritual people suffer and only people with an important call on their life have to go through truly difficult things. Yet I would watch people suffer over and over and think perhaps God was cruel. My paradigm wasn't quite right.

In this move of God that is upon us, God is looking for those who will manifest His love. Our trapped emotions and irrational belief systems will keep an open door for Satan to keep us in our flesh and offended. This will be about **1 Corinthians 13:4-8: "** *Love is patient, love is kind and is not jealous; love does not brag and is not arrogant, does not act unbecomingly; it does not seek its own, is not provoked, does not take into account a wrong suffered, does not rejoice in unrighteousness, but rejoices with the truth; bears all things,* *believes all things, hopes all things, endures all things. Love never fails.* When I read this, it occurs to me that I am uncapable of this kind of love. This verse is filled with so many opportunities for offense and triggered trapped emotions. It occurs to me that to manifest this kind of love, I must focus on getting my unconscious belief aligned with what God says about me and others so that the Holy Spirit can flow through me without blockages. This is my message – if you want to change the world then get unblocked, get joyful, get peaceful as these are the conditions of our being for God to use us to change the world.

Understanding the Law of Attraction has created a new understanding of "ask, seek and knock." (**Matthew 7:7**). Since I have chosen to move towards believing God is for me and that I have favor with men and God, my life has been more peaceful and I continue to move towards a deeper trust in my relationship with the Lord and fulfill His call on my life with great joy and expectation.

So I invite you to reread the "to do" list again and again and make a strategy of change. This will require you to make time to do so on a daily basis. Changes are best done a little at time if you want to maintain them. New Year's resolutions rarely work because our brains are not wired to accept radical change easily. Sit down and write out a 3-month plan of daily, weekly and monthly changes you want to make and be diligent to do them daily (but don't quit if you miss a day or two). Talk to some people and ask them to hold you accountable to make these changes. Do whatever it takes to truly implement them. Read and reread and self educate to remind yourself that you believe in these spiritual laws and the Law of Attraction. If you and I are the only ones to apply these principles and change, then, based on the principles of the Law of Attraction, we have changed the world. **Would you become a cheerleader with me?**

As a P.S., recently I was awakened at 3 am by an intense presence of the Lord. These visitations have been very powerful in my life mostly because my brain is shut off and so the voice of the Lord is crystal clear to me. Some of the most powerful revelations from Him have come in these 3 am experiences. On this occasion, the Lord said this to me, "There is a new anointing of the Holy Spirit coming now. Remember that the Spirit who spoke the world into existence is a force of intense creative power. Everything you think and say will matter. You can have whatever you can imagine and believe. I will give authority to those who are deliberate about what they think, say and feel because I can trust them to cocreate with Me in ways that will advance the Kingdom. Whatever you can imagine can be created and manifested." Imagine if the Lord woke you and told you that whatever you imagined, desired and thought about intensely would manifest. This is what the Law of Attraction states, but what if God visited you and told you this personally? Would you believe this? Does that sound too good to be true? How to would your life be different if you really believed every thought mattered and your thoughts were powerful enough to change the world?

This is the message with which I have been passionately imbued, commissioned and share wherever I go. In this next season of transformation, the outpouring of the Glory of God will involve a level of power in our words and thoughts that will manifest signs, miracles and wonders. We can disqualify ourselves by staying in a worldly mindset of judgments, gossip and offense or we can decide we have been called and commissioned to change the world. Like Nehemiah, we can choose to not be swayed to come down off the wall. We can stay focused on the mission to change the world through forgiveness, repentance and blessing; through thinking only on the glorious possibilities that God can achieve and manifest in any situation and in any person (vs the negative "reality"). If we can co-create a new reality, lets get going!

TO FIND OUT MORE ABOUT THE AUTHOR, GO TO INTEGRATEDLIFESTRATEGIES.COM.

Robin Perry Braun does individual sessions for emotional release and creating new beliefs as well as coaching on lifestyle changes that raise your vibration and create a healthier holistic lifestyle without losing life quality.

Christian Corporations and Churches can experience renewal when the core leadership goes through personal and corporate intensives. Her corporate transformation plan shows the team how their life beliefs, judgments and trapped emotions affect the whole based on the spiritual principles of the leadership.

She also co-teaches **"Wholly Healed Workshops"** which are focused on holistic and integrated principles of wellness and living a life as a son of God.

She is available as a speaker for church services or workshops. Topics can be tailored to the purposes of the meeting.

Contact is available on the website or by emailing her at:

Integratedlifestrategies@gmail.com

Endnotes

[i] Per Wikipedia

[ii] *http://www.selfgrowth.com/articles/The_Law_of_Attraction_Quantum_P hysics.html*

[iii] From James Allen, As a Man Thinketh (Best Success Books, orig. 1902, republished 2010)

[iv] Per Kevin Trudeau tapes series, Wish is Your Command (Global Information Network (2009)

[v] **http://cellphonesafety.wordpress.com/2006/09/17/the-frequency-of-the-human-bodyand-your-coffee/**

[vi] David R Hawkins, M.D., Ph.D., Power Vs Force (Carlsbad, CA: Hay House, Inc.) 1995, 1998, 2002, 2012

[vii] **http://www.fengshuidana.com/wp-content/uploads/2012/11/water20pics1.jpg**

[viiiviii] Rhonda Byrne, *The Secret,* (Hillsborough, Oregon: Beyond Words Publishing) 2006

[ix] Per Kevin Trudeau tape series

[x] Hill, Napoleon; Cornwell, Ross, Think *and Grow Rich! The Original Version Revised* (San Diego, CA: Aventine Press, 2004 – original 1937)

[xi] James Allen.

[xii] Dr. George Burriss, II Ph.D., Munger Place Church, Dallas, TX

[xiii] Allan N. Schore, M.D., *Affect Regulation the Origin of Self: The neurobiology of Emotional Development* (Hillsborough, NJ, Lawrence Erlbaum Associates, Inc.) 1994

[xiv] E James Wilder, Et al, *The Life Model, Living from the Heart Jesus Gave You* (Los Angeles, CA: Shepherds House, Inc.) 2000

[xv] **http://en.wikipedia.org/wiki/Karma**

[xvixvi] Kerry Kirkwood, *The Power of Blessing*, (Shippensburg, PA: Destiny Image Publishers, Inc.) 2010

[xvii] Per Kevin Trudeau tape series,

[xviii] Per Dr. George Burriss's teaching

[xix] Per Strong's Concordance

[xx] **http://www.mindbodygreen.com/0-11982/7-scientific-reasons-you-should-listen-to-your-heart-not-your-brain.html**

[xxi] **http://www.whydontyoutrythis.com/2013/06/scientists-prove-dna-can-be-reprogrammed-by-words-and-frequencies.html?m=1**

[xxii] **http://www.merriam-webster.com/dictionary/prodigal**

[xxiii] http://EzineArticles.com/6111179

[xxivxxiv] Per Wikipedia

[xxv] Napoleon Hill

[xxvi] Gary Chapman, The Five Love Languages, (Chicago, IL: Northfield Publishing)2010

[xxvii] Alex Loyd, *The Healing Code*,(Peoria, AZ: Intermediary Publishing Group) 2010